How I Met the Man of My Dreams
a guide to MANifesting yours

by Debbianne DeRose

How I Met the Man of My Dreams
a guide to MANifesting yours

Published by PiscAquarian Press

PiscAQUARIAN
PRESS

www.debbianne.com

Cover design by Lynda Mangoro, creative genius.
Interior illustrations by Debbianne DeRose
and by Anthony Scarpelos, Dreamboat.
Sean Hayes lyrics reprinted by permission and with thanks.

ISBN 978-0-9854101-3-1

Set in Didot and Heartthings.
Paper sourcing certified by
the Forest Stewardship Council™ (FSC®) and
Sustainable Forestry Initiative® (SFI®).

this one's for the sisterhood

With love,
Debbianne

HOW I MET THE MAN OF MY DREAMS:
a guide to MANifesting yours

ALLOW ME

to explain...

*"Well I wait so long for my love vibration
and I'm dancing with myself."*
—Billy Idol

Perhaps you can relate. I'd been single for

so damn long that it started looking grim—like I was on a long bumpy road headed straight for Spinster City. But I'd sooner take a cliff-dive drive, Thelma-and-Louise style, than reach *that* destination.

I had become a camel, plodding across the Love Desert, expertly rationing my supplies between oases. I suppose I'd gotten fairly used to trekking solo. Nonetheless, a camel needs a *hump*. I subsisted on whatever wellsprings were available—those romantic flings arising unpredictably, however fleeting and unsatisfying they may have been. But the aqueous offerings grew more meager with each passing year. Thirsty times in the midlife love-drought, I tell you.

Being as picky as I am, most men simply didn't qualify as relationship material. My standards were simultaneously being raised *and* lowered because, while my spec sheet for Mr. Right was morphing into a half-ton opus, the less I knew about Mr. Right Now, the better. At one point I insisted aloud to the Universe that all I really wanted was someone who wouldn't annoy me for a weekend. I honestly could not imagine or believe there was a man alive capable of measuring up to my seemingly lofty ideals.

Former fairytale optimism regarding love-at-first-sight sightings and "best friends as lovers" schemes had been all but squelched through years of post-divorce living. That delicious experience of full-on chemical merging, in all its physical, emotional and spiritual splendor, was reduced to a vaguer-than-vague distant memory. Of course, there was the occasional mirage, thanks to my indomitable twin-powers of delusion and desperation: a sure-as-shit Mr. Wrong masquerading as a suitable suitor. But hey, it's easy to get waylaid on the path—especially if you're getting way laid.

Despite all the romantic doom and gloom, some part of me knew I was biding my time. Namely, the unclouded part that watches over the fumbling part and smirks knowingly. Apparently this part started flexing her smartypants muscle more often, as I became drawn to all manner of "woo-woo," metaphysical, spiritual, and self-improvement material. It's mostly *What I Did On My Midlife Crisis Vacation*, as a matter of fact and shockingly, a lot of it actually contributed to an improved self.

Then one day, it happened. Mr. Right On walked onto the set, emerging from the murky ethers! 'Twas a glorious, mind-blowing thing, and I was deer-in-the-headlights incredulous at first, dumbstruck and lovestruck all at once. I mean, this man had all of the qualities I sought—and then some—embodied in one stellar male meatsuit. It was like winning the Love Lottery without ever buying a ticket.

A whirlwind tryst ensued, but I knew right away it wasn't just another oasis destined to evaporate once he revealed his gapingly unacceptable flaws (never mind my own). Oh no, this was something else—the real deal, the whole enchilada. That heretofore-elusive but magnificent, exalted Thunderclap of Love.

One week later, I was still pinching myself when I realized just how accurate all those metaphysical teachings had been. Plus there was a new twist to my understanding: it's not actually necessary to fully believe or even be able to visualize the complete end-product of your desire. My crisis of imagination, it turns out, was not fatal.

3

It also became plain that certain old ruts of mine had stalled the big MANifestation while other, newly acquired habitudes hastened it. And so, I'm inspired to share all these insights with the single sistren. I'm pretty sure *your* journey can be shortened and lightened by hearing about mine. The combination of my acute hindsight and your self-inflicted kindsight could be downright diabolical.

I've synthesized a variety of information, interpreting it all with the aid of my personal 'aha!' collection and seasoning the curation with wacky humor, tough love, and a pop culture garnish. May it please your self-help palette.

My major influences include: Bashar and Darryl Anka, Abraham-Hicks, Louise Hay, Jack Canfield, Rick Stack, Seth and Jane Roberts, Sanaya Roman and Duane Packer, Sonia Choquette, the fabulous Dooley brothers, Robert Monroe, and Marianne Williamson, plus other modern seers and many of the classic "new thought" authors of yesteryear. This stuff pertains to everything in life, not just MANifesting a SupraLove, and has the overarching potential to guide you in transforming yourself into a happier, more self-fulfilled human. It's win-win, all the way.

Before we go any further though, we should probably make sure we're roughly on the same page.

Let's Make a Deal, Shall We?

How we think about Life seems to fall into a few broad categories. That's not to say that most people fit squarely in one camp or another, but here are the primary views:

© 2013 Debbianne DeRose

1. Shit just happens.
This is the defeatist manifesto. Life is random; often it sucks, and that's just the way things are. If good shit happens to you, well you simply got lucky, but there's no rhyme or reason to it.

2. Shit was meant to happen (or not).
Life is preordained or scripted somehow, by Fate or God or Karma or faerie-elfin friends. Or maybe Fate is ad-libbing this shit, but basically we, as puny human beings, don't have much of a clue or a say in it.

3. We make shit happen.
We're powerful. Life is a reflection of what's going on within us. We can consciously choose to change ourselves, and therefore, experience different shit.

Behind Door No. 3 is *empowerment*. That unlikely provider of mantras, George Dubya Bush, was known to proudly profess, "I am the Decider." And while he probably meant it for everyone else, I sometimes co-opt the phrase to remind myself that yes, *I am the dictator of my own reality.* Aligning unconscious dictates with conscious preferences is the ultimate personal coup d'etat.

I must admit, there are times when I wonder if a suite between rooms 2 and 3 might be closer to the Truth. I mean, maybe there *is* a detailed master plan for my life and I'm just an Earthbound puppet, convinced that I'm acting on free will (snicker snicker). Well, if that's the case, and Free Will is but a big cosmic practical joke, it's one hell of an airtight illusion because this deliberate manifesting stuff *works*. So even if there *is* an in-depth master plan, it must be true that our earthly desires are simpatico with it, and we might as well proceed as if we're calling the shots.

I bring all this up not necessarily to spur elaborate deliberations about the great mysteries of Life, but to point out this basic premise: if you happen to be stationed behind one of the first two doors with six deadbolts thrown and a sawed-off shotgun in your hands, you aren't likely to get much out of this book. In other words, if you insist that *my* MANifestation is the product of dumb luck or sufficient karma points saved up from other lifetimes like so many S&H Green Stamps, how can I possibly help you to help yourself?

In all likelihood, you feel drawn to Door No. 3 but perhaps a little skittish about stepping inside. Great, then! You've come to the right place.

Cue the Woo

Time to interject a definition for the under-initiated. "Woo" or "woo-woo" is a flippantly affectionate term for anything outside the domain of the logical ego-brain and its five-sense minions—particularly, all that is mystical, metaphysical, paranormal, "spiritual", or New Agey. Probably it's been derived from the Chinese word "Wu" but that's an etymology project for another day.

You may encounter other lingual weirdnesses in these pages, for it is my great joy to remain true to my weird self via written expression. I apologize for your inconvenience or head-scratching should it occur, but please don't hesitate to drop me a line via my website to demand explanations as needed. Or ask your old friend, The Google, what it thinks. Or check out the Urban Dictionary for fun takes on things.

Okay, so back to Planet Woo-Woo. Despite that bout of metaphysical amnesia between notable MANifestations in my life, I've been down with the Wu for decades; the foundation was poured long before my recent luxuriant homecoming. But my desert-wandering phase was far from pointless. It taught me how to do things the hard way so I could fully comprehend the difference. Duality and *contrast*, it turns out, are highly useful devices for learning and expanding, even though we often curse them in frustration. There is always light at the end of the tunnel... and more tunnels to slip into, if we so choose.

Back in the 1980s, I was very open to possibilities— largely unconstrained by the mental calluses of doubt and cynicism that so often come with age. An extraordinary high school friend turned me on to the then-radical notion that *thoughts create circumstances*. She demonstrated it through her personal life, and handed me a number of seminal books by Louise Hay, Marc Allen, Shakti Gawain and other mover-shakers of that era. With typical Jersey girl tough-love, she inscribed one with a message that I've never forgotten: "You've got to *know* what you want before you can get it." Being picky is actually a very helpful thing.

Casually but enthusiastically, I assembled my first Vision Board collage, or Treasure Map as Shakti Gawain called them. Creating it was as natural as breathing for me, as I'd spent a good portion of my childhood holed up in my room, consumed by one artsy-craftsy project or another. The focus was—you guessed it—a MANifestation. My requirements were relatively few and centered on his physical appearance and musical tastes, to be perfectly honest. (Therein lies the beauty of aging: *refined preference*.) Fortunately for me, the list tallied by the Universe on our behalf is always far more intricate than whatever we're currently focused on.

Afterward, my collage was quickly buried under a pile of papers, and I spent approximately zero hours and minutes worrying about whether or not it might come true. I was busy living my life, and having a swell time of it.

Two months later, I quit my job and drove across country with scant possessions and bold plans of attending graduate school in Berserkeley once I established California residency. I had saved a modest amount of cash, which disappeared more quickly than I'd thought possible, but I was conspicuously carefree about it all. As we grow older, we tend to have more of everything—including the fear of losing it. Sometimes that fear prevents us from starting something new, as our minds race to some potential future

8

loss or failure. But such fearful notions were fairly alien to me at that age. They simply never crossed my mind.

Not even 48 hours after my tires crossed the Golden State line, I just *happened* to meet a man who matched my Treasure Map to a tee—the man I would later marry—and we began our warp-speed courting process. My non-woowoo friends were astounded at the speed and accuracy of this so-called "law of attraction" funny business. Yes, he and I later went our separate ways, but don't let that dampen your enthusiasm. After all, I was young and, unbeknownst to me at the time, had a motherlode of changing to do. To each era its own MANifestation, I say. Life is a sort of bottomless cookie jar, once you're able to transcend the self-imposed limitations that insist otherwise.

During my mid-thirties, post-divorce Oregon era, I constructed another Man-collage—a big one, with sultry images and pithy phrases plucked from various print media. This time I hung it on my bedroom wall, pleased with my artwork for art's sake, and not feeling particularly urgent about the MANifesting part of things. In other words, I didn't obsess over the fact that it hadn't yet materialized. I went about living my life—again, mostly free of worrisome thoughts. Smack dab in the center of that cut-and-paste wonderland was the phrase, "Don't worry, he'll find you."

One evening a few months later, while I was getting ready to attend one of those epic Portland theme parties, my party-going pal called to inform me that his housemate would be joining us at my place before the party. Soon after, there was a knock on the front door, and I swung it open to reveal Mr. Tall, Dark, Handsome, Fun and Oh-So-Young on my doorstep. There was instant chemical attraction. After the party, we stayed up 'til dawn chatting away, and he returned the following night for a proper date. And the next day. And

9

the next, leading to a mojo-infusing life-affirming love affair that matched my vision board in every possible way. And it couldn't have been more effortless, since he literally did "find me." *Nice touch, Universe.*

So, yeah, this woo-woo shit actually works. And it works whether or not you make a formal hearts-and-flowers poster-board project out of it. It might even work better if you *don't*. It all depends on your unique mind, and getting to know your own mind is the key to MANifesting.

The truth is that each one of us is a living, breathing transmitter and receiver of signals—a sophisticated human cell phone, if you will. Round the clock, our desires, complaints and observations gush forth in a constant stream of vibration that gets beamed back to us in the form of manifestations *in every moment of our experience.*

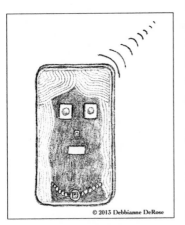
© 2013 Debbianne DeRose

Most people adopt the habit of "offering thought," as Abraham-Hicks describes it, in response to what they're observing, rather than shaping thought in accordance with what they are wanting. Their mental commentary is mostly negative, reinforcing unwanted conditions over and over again as they recycle the same thought-signals. Why? Because it's what nearly everybody else does—like having babies or driving a car, or even just breathing. It's an unconscious way of living, and a very common way at that. It may seem natural to mentally or verbally comment on what you observe, but I don't think Nature intended for us to ever stray so far from our bliss.

Anything can *seem* natural and normal when you experience it on a constant basis, and that includes dysfunction.

If the life you're living is unsatisfactory, you've been sending out mixed messages—conducting multiple simultaneous phone conversations with the Universe (not to mention talkin' smack). If change is what you're after, you need to unify your broadcast and quit muddying up the signals with thoughts that contradict your preferences. It's not so much what you *need to do* as it is what you *need to stop doing*. The experience of happiness, love and abundance is actually the default Life design. It's already available; you just need to clean out the debris that's blocking your view.

My friend Cindy and I were having a girl-tawk luncheon one day when the topic of MANifesting came up. "Oh yeah, I know all about the Law of Attraction (LOA)—I watched 'The Secret' a few times," she quipped dismissively. Only five minutes later she was lamenting her degrading eyesight and telling me how she requires a stronger prescription all the time. Now, I'm not about to play Metaphysical Police, nor do I lack compassion for others and their health concerns, but I share this story to illustrate a point: people tend to view this stuff as a *project* to enlist when they're feeling inspired to "manifest" something special in their lives, while remaining relatively oblivious to their everyday, ongoing thought-creations. Most people agree that thoughts do *influence* our experiences, but *only* in selective situations and *only* to the degree that their rational minds feel comfortable.

News flash: it doesn't work that way. Either this LOA thing is on, or it isn't—period. I happen to know that it *is* on, round the clock, and that's why we call it a Law, not an option or suggestion. And although I like to use phrases like "Man-project" or refer to a MANifestation as a succinct event or person, I'm only having fun with words. *Manifesting is synonymous with living.* We're doing it all the time, and we can never stop doing it. *Conscious manifesting* is a particular *way* of living—a decision to wake up, take charge, and bushwhack a new path for yourself. Does that sound difficult or scary? It doesn't need to be. It's actually incredibly rewarding and fun, once you get rolling.

That film, *The Secret,* was all the rage a few years ago, but how many people change their lives after watching it? Why is it that some people hear the Truth, nod in agreement, then walk away and resume their self-sabotaging activities? The short answer is: the ego-intellect. When the ego-based mind can't figure things out, it tends to put the kibosh on the whole process. But when the rational intellect oversteps its authority, you have the option of setting it straight. That's because *you* are so much more than just your rational mind.

Ultimately, what motivates people to take the ball and run with it is their *knowing*, beyond the shadow of a doubt, that the Law of Attraction is real and is in effect 24/7. Once you *know*—really know—that your thoughts form the blueprint of your experience, you become motivated and determined to improve the selection of those thoughts. But for most people, the cause-and-effect cycle is convoluted.

By way of analogy, imagine that cars were designed with the exhaust pipe in the center of the steering wheel, rather than out the back end. There would be some major changes in fuel-burning, and fast! The fact that we are distanced in time and space from the effects of our mind-pollution is what enables us to keep readily emitting and ignoring it.

No one can ever *prove to you* that the Law of Attraction is real—that all of Life, every single iota of it, is governed by the principle of What-You-Put-Out-Is-What-You-Get-Back. The only way to *know* it is to prove it to yourself through direct personal experience.

In the absence of knowing, there is *belief* or *faith* to fall back on—sufficient to motivate some people, but not others. What about you? Can you muster enough momentum to persevere by borrowing enthusiasm from others like me, or are you going to be a tougher nut to crack?

If you're the skeptical type, you *must* find a way to generate some evidence for yourself, and you must find a way to obtain the cooperation of your analytical mind in order to begin creating that evidence in the first place. Hey, look, I'm no stranger to skepticism, and I think it's quite healthy, to a degree. But I also know what it's like to be held hostage by the Intellect. It can put up insidious detour signs on your Man-project road trip, leaving you stranded somewhere in the desert with a flat tire when you *could* be rolling down Lover's Lane. The ego is a sneaky bastard at times—not *evil*, because nothing really is, but, perhaps more like a misbehaving child in need of love and a little discipline. It pays to have a plan for circumvention.

What *doesn't* usually pay is launching theoretical tangents examining cause-and-effect in the lives of others, tempting as that may be. It may not even be fruitful to analyze your own Past, past a certain point. The ego-intellect may seek to "disprove" the Law of Attraction and effectively arrest your progress that way. It means well, of course. It's just trying to keep you safe and in line with your unconscious belief systems. We'll be examining those sacred cows… and clearing the manure from our minds.

The best thing to do, in my opinion, is to embark on a brand new *empirical* study of your own devising. In other words, become your own lab rat. Strike a deal with your cerebral self that you will be conducting an experiment of finite duration, during which time you agree to play by the rules, *acting as if your thought-emanations, and yours alone, create your life experience,* whether or not you truly think so at this point. If you're fond of science, hear this: collecting data while harboring an unstated bias is not very scientific. If you're assuming LOA is bunk from the onset, your data will be skewed and your conclusions will support that bias.

Commit to *suspending disbelief.* Your willingness to proceed is all that's needed—I'll help you with the rest.

If you encounter ideas that induce squirming, don't allow your ego to claim this as a valid excuse for dropping out. If you automatically reject things because they don't jibe with your current belief systems, you're doing yourself a grand disservice. The ego-intellect has been trained to sort things into categories labeled "this OR that", forcing you to decide, for instance, that this book is either "good" or "bad". Well, maybe it's *both* for you. Consider adopting a "this AND that" approach to life. You can allow paradox to stick around if you release the need to reach conclusions prematurely.

In what seems like lifetimes ago, I attended corporate staff meetings in which unresolvable-for-now items were placed on a dedicated big-paper easel labeled "Parking Lot Issues." You might want to borrow this technique for your own purposes: park your disbelief and mental blocks in the lot, and stay on the road to the MANifestival. Your ability to entertain new ideas and act upon them—and to lighten up and have fun while doing it—will take you far.

Begin now to *intend* for a smooth ride. This requires no effort on your part—only a slight shift in mindset. Intention is a very powerful thing, and you'll want to get into the habit of "pre-paving" your experiences with positive expectation.

I highly recommend keeping a journal to catch all the little things that come up. Like subtle changes or synchronicities that occur, and how you're feeling and dealing with shit that comes up, whether you define it as "good," "bad" or otherwise. It's easy to forget these interim baby-steps soon after they occur, but that's actually the juicy part needed for understanding how this Law of Attraction stuff works. Glossed-over accounts we sometimes read and hear are nice ("I wanted something... and then it magically showed up!"), but realistic details of the emotional journey are the key to thoroughly inspiring others—including yourself—later on.

My job in all of this is to help you *re-mind yourself* of what you already know, as an eternal being, deep down inside. Not everything I say will resonate with every reader, but this little book is so chock full of metaphors, analogies, examples, and alternate angles on the core issues that sooner or later *something* is bound to click for *you*.

I remain a relentless cheerleader for your happiness, because I happen to know that you *can* have anything you desire—including, and especially, the Man of Your Dreams. It's never too late, and you're never too old or too *anything* (except possibly too stubborn) for your dreams to come true.

> "*As you learn to accept your vibrational nature and begin to consciously utilize your emotional vibrational indicators, you will gain conscious control of your personal creations and of the outcomes of your life experience.*"
> —*Abraham-Hicks*

Next up, for your inspiration: a Love Story. We'll analyze it later on, when we dive headlong into the Woo, but for now let's just have fun unfurling it. Use it to fuel the spinning of your own magical Love Tale, however similar or divergent yours may be.

MONROMANCE

a multi-dimensional love story

Two years before we met, I felt his arm around me as I lay in bed one morning. It wasn't a dream, as I was wide awake and alert, having trained myself to remain motionless for the sake of enhancing my dream recall. Of course, at the time, I had no idea whose arm it was. Nor did I necessarily believe it was somehow emanating energetically from a particular person. (I hadn't gotten quite so woo-woo yet.) I only knew that it felt good to be spooned after countless months of sleeping alone. The fact that it was merely a flash-in-the-pan phantom spooner didn't spoil my fun in the least.

Within a week of that strangeness, another sign of him appeared. I'd been experimenting with various healing modalities ever since a I'd learned that I created a big ol' cyst on my left ovary. During one long distance energy healing session, I lay comfortably on my bed, anticipating some sort of kinesthetic pyrotechnics. In that relaxed state, a striking image crawled into my mind's eye of a man and woman holding hands. Between and all around them was an exquisitely beautiful, sparkly celestial backdrop—as if the energy between them formed some sort of portal or force field or something. (This book's cover is an artist's rendition of it.) The visual was accompanied by feelings of sweet satisfaction—of love, otherworldly and pure.

It was nothing like I'd expected, this energy work session —nothing much to report, kinesthetically. But I suppose we always get what we *need*. I felt lighter afterward, and used the incident as my permission slip to slip those SupraLove files out of the "Probably Never Again" folder and into the one labeled "Maybe, just Maybe."

About a year later, I set out on a road trip, back home to California from Texas where I had just indulged myself in acquiring the Car of My Dreams—a hard-to-find modern

Love Buggie. The cute thing had spent its entire life in the Lonestar State, having barely made it across the border from Mexico where it had been born into a small litter. It had been an undeniable case of Love at First Sight via the Interweb. But I hadn't owned a car in nearly two decades, so it was kind of a big deal for me. I was embracing change left and right.

As a travel-addict, this car-fetching shenanigan was also a good excuse to tour the southwest. The UFO museum in Roswell, New Mexico was fascinating, as were the stupendous sweeping mesa-views and cloudscapes they have down there that are just ripe for the ogling.

After a white-knuckled drive across a snowy pass or two, I concluded Day Two of my solo trek, retiring for the night in Sedona, Arizona. Visually spectacular, and well nigh irresistible to outdoor jocks, Sedona is also known in woo-woo circles for its legendary "vortex" energy. There were probably more touristy signs hawking "Spiritual Vortex Tours" than there were residents. Normally I go in for that sort of thing—for the writing fodder if nothing else—but the next morning, I just wasn't in the mood. So I started making my way out of town while drinking in the epic scenery that was one part rocky desert and two parts winter wonderland.

All of a sudden, just as I was about to hop on the main highway, I got inspired to turn around. I'd passed a whole slew of metaphysical shops peddling books and crystals and New Age chotchkes, but one of them had stood out and lingered in my mind. So I went back to investigate. At this point in my life, I knew better than to ignore such intuitive promptings.

Inside the shop, I was greeted by Elizabeth, the confident, warm and matter-of-fact proprietress. I felt a growing desire for a tarot card reading, which is something I like to do every now and again. But initially I balked at her prices, which were high even by California standards. I endured a brief hemming-and-hawing session while browsing her impressive geode collection, then figured, "oh, what the hell. I was drawn here for a reason, and I just spent a shit-ton of money on the car, so why not blow a little more on this?" Carpe diem wins again.

Elizabeth asked me to shuffle the cards briefly, then she drew a modest spread. She spoke glowingly of my writing and described visions of me helping other women to empower themselves. It was exciting, bolstering stuff to hear. I think that's the beauty and value of a psychic reading: permission to feel better about yourself, your life and all its potential. So what if their predictions don't come to fruition? It's how you *feel* in the Now that truly matters. And it's that good-feeling state which actually enables the fruit to ripen—whether it's that same "apple" the psychic is talking about, or some "orange" of your own design.

Somewhere in the middle of the reading, Elizabeth slapped *The Lovers* card on top of the others, as she let out a little gasp, then stared into realms unknown. After a momentary pause, she described a magnificent love affair that I was soon to take part in. "There will be a great deal of freedom..." she asserted, "and it may be a long-distance thing." Oh, and it had *something* to do with my book.

Provocative ideas, to say the least. I must admit that I had, in fact, been periodically fantasizing that one day I'd meet an amazing man who had read my memoir, knew a lot about me, and was nevertheless enthralled, so he'd made it his mission in Life to meet me. Sure, it's an ego-riffic fantasy, but hey, whatever gets you through the night. Maybe

I was just being efficient; if he read my story, then I wouldn't need to explain myself.

It was a fond reverie, but I swiftly snapped out of it. After all, I'd heard similar predictions to no material avail. It wasn't the first time that sneaky *Lovers* card showed up to taunt me. And the card reader always seemed to say "about three months..." if I inquired when I might meet this alleged Lover Man. It was beginning to sound like a canned program.

It's not that the psychics were necessarily wrong (and I speak of the genuine variety, not the phonies). It's just that the Future is an infinite set of options, and we've got freedom of choice, so they're only working with probabilities. And since I'd been making so many radical turns the last few years, my swervy reality-path wasn't all that predictable. Later on, I would come to see that I could have met the Man of My Dreams sooner, had I understood vibrational Resistance and the need to release it. So if the psychics were relaying potential in me that I failed to realize, I'm the one to be held accountable, not them.

By the time I met Elizabeth in Sedona, I was fairly stable. I'd been studying the Abraham-Hicks material intently for half a year, and was committed to maintaining my own happiness, come hell or high water. So I allowed Elizabeth's words to lift my mood a bit higher, but not so much as to rock the boat. Mostly, I remained blissfully indifferent... and got back on the road for more Love Buggie adventures.

Back home and following my bliss as usual, I continued to read self-help books and watch various programs, often in metaphysical chain-smoking fashion—one idea or author leads to another, and another. If there's something I apparently need to pay closer attention to, I usually get some sort of extrasensory nudge. In one of those cosmic pokings, I suddenly became consumed with the idea that I could, should, and would return to the Monroe Institute (TMI) in Virginia—this time, for the Guidelines program.

I'd already completed three residential programs at the Institute so I was becoming something of a Monroe junkie. Which is easy to do. It's a unique place, founded by the late Robert A. Monroe as an incubator for assisted self-exploration of consciousness. Their well-crafted fun weeklong programs utilize hemispheric synchronization (or hemi-sync) sound frequencies to facilitate participants' discoveries that they are much *more than their physical bodies*. Bob Monroe was famous for his Out-of-Body Experience (OBE) research. And though I hadn't yet experienced the classic OBE myself, I'd had some major personal breakthroughs there and wrote about them in my memoir. There's really nothing quite like TMI, and it's always a treat to return to my woo-woo home-away-from-home.

I chose the Guidelines program this time, amongst their diverse offerings, because I was in career mode. My book was about to be published and I was wondering what my next step might be. A week dedicated to inner guidance (via spirit helpers, higher self, or however you prefer to conceive of it) seemed like the perfect thing.

With my self-made happiness plan in effect, I was inwardly focused and selectively social... and more satisfied with my life than ever before. The fact that a shift had taken place within me became particularly poignant on the first day of the new year.

The night before, at a New Year's Eve dance, I'd passed on the opportunity to "hang out" with a fellow dancer afterward. He was coming on strong, and I liked him well enough, but I thought, "well, if there is something more than drunken horniness to this attraction, it can wait. He can ask me out at the next dance." He never did, and the next time I saw him he was hitting on another chick—and avoiding eye contact with me. I was feeling righteously sovereign, and loving toward them both—not at all rejected or angry as the younger me might have felt.

There was another dancing man I'd developed a friendship with and a crush on, and he didn't even bother to show up at the dance (and it wasn't the first time he'd done so). Observing his cycle of flakiness with new clarity, I suddenly resolved, once and for all, to nix him as a prospect. Any fantasies involving him were thereby declared defunct. Self-assured like never before, I simply was not willing to accept any more lame dudes. I can honestly say I was content being single and solo on New Year's Eve.

That was right around the time I got an email from my friend Maria Conlon. It was a relatively rare occurrence, as I didn't have very much contact with her. Not that I wouldn't care to, but it's just the way things were at the time. She's one of those uber-powerful, tuned-in women who does energy healing for a living. So when I got this message from her out of the blue, I was quite curious.

She was writing to let me know she had received a sudden and unmistakable "download" that a man was coming into *my* life—and soon. Well! I got a little excited, I must admit.

And yet, being prone to skepticism and unwilling to compromise my hard-earned high vibration with a possible future letdown, I relegated it to the "would be nice... but still hard to believe" category and got back to work.

Then a funny thing happened. As I settled in to my editing project, I heard something clanking underneath my desk. My workspace had gotten a bit out of control while I feverishly worked to complete the book, and it looked as if a cyclone had swept through. But…what the hell was making that sound? *Papers don't clank*. I crawled underneath to solve the mystery, and unearthed a pewter metal contraption with a handle and a lid—a curious antique that I'd picked up at a thrift store, but long since forgotten and left for dead.

I opened the lid to discover a stack of business cards living in there. On top was Maria's! Uh-huh. *Now* things were getting *really* interesting. I felt as if some spirit guide was elbowing me in the ribs: "Pay attention to her—she knows what she's talking about."

Incidentally, that pewter antique, I'm told, is actually a *bed warmer*.

January 20th found me in high spirits and high above the earth, at cruising altitude. I was Virginia-bound, eager to satisfy both my traveling jones and my woo-woo addiction in one fell swoop.

I always feel a certain giddiness at the start of a Monroe Institute program—a magical openness to possibilities. You never know where the consciousness tour bus will drop you off, or who'll be on board, but you can pretty much guarantee a remarkable ride. The idea that I might meet a Lover Man there had occurred to me before—indeed it was one of my favorite fantasies. The reason I even knew about TMI was from reading Frank DeMarco's memoir, *Muddy Tracks*, which is all about his amazing experiences during and as a result of Monroe programs—including *astral sex*. The prospects of it intrigued me to no end, and if ever there was a place to meet someone weird enough to be into astral sex, TMI was it.

What exactly *is* astral sex, you ask? You know how people often say that we only use five percent of our brains? Well, I figured "doing it" on the astral plane must be like using the entirety of your brain, firing on all cylinders so to speak, while remaining completely aware of everything. But I was just guessing. Other people's accounts are fascinating, but the only way to truly know what it's about is to experience it firsthand. So astral sex became one of my paramount aims in life—a high priority on my woo-woo bucket list. The idea of experiencing shared reality with another in alternate realms or dimensions was exciting enough, but then you add in sex and, well... how does it get any better than that?

My adorable friend Jolanda picked me up at the Charlottesville airport, and we spent a fun 24 hours catching up prior to the start of my program. She and I had met at a Monroe program the year before, and we instantly bonded. It was yet another episode in my life of long lost soul sisters, joyfully reunited. It became tradition to meet up with her before and after I went to the Institute.

Our current cackle-fest was drawing to a close, as she drove me up the hill on which the TMI buildings are perched. Jolie turned to me suddenly and blurted out, "You know what? I think you're going to meet someone!" She had that goose-bump thing that accompanies truth-from-beyond dispatches in many a woo-woo person.

By this time I was more willing than ever to entertain the thought, probably because the verdict was near. There was no possibility of dragging out suspense while my fantasies expanded unstably, filling up like an emotional hot-air balloon only to crash-land in DisappointmentVille later on.

I let Jolie in on my preoccupation with astral sex and to my surprise, she responded with a juicy story about a former Lover Man of hers. They'd met at the Monroe Institute, as a matter of fact, and while lying in their respective beds and rooms during a hemi-sync exercise, they both expanded beyond their physical bodies and merged in the astral plane. It was a sort of cosmic coitus before anything was actually happening between them in the "normal" physical world. Talk about starting off with a bang. Better still, it had happened during Guidelines—the very program I was about to begin—in the very building we were now pulling up to. More thrill chills!

Continuing the giddy girl-chat, we walked around the building where I would be sleeping, eating, socializing, and expanding my consciousness for the next six days: the Nancy Penn Center, dedicated by the late Bob Monroe to his beloved second wife. Portraits of the lovebirds hung proudly on the foyer walls, forever facing each other.

Upon opening that familiar front door, the first person I laid eyes on was a good-looking guy about my age who was engrossed in conversation in the hallway. He paused for a round of introductions, and I couldn't help but notice his decisive, warm handshake in stark contrast to the other guy's tentative, noodley grasp. Tony was his name. His smile alone could move mountains, and it was already inciting an endorphin rumble in my cells.

I dropped off my bags, then Jolie and I went back outside, presumably for a refill of crisp mountain air and scenery, but mainly to explode into giggles about the eye candy we'd just witnessed inside. "Tony's your man!" she gushed insistently. But I wasn't so sure, and slightly embarrassed that she'd said it so loudly. I wasn't ready to jump to any premature conclusions.

Jolie spent a few minutes surveying the grounds and reminiscing, then we parted company with long hugs and more grins and giggles, planning to reconvene at the end of the week... that is, unless something else came up.

Back inside the cozy Nancy Penn Center, I unpacked and met my roommate, Nicole, a fun sassy German woman who was training to become a Monroe outreach instructor. Soon I made a beeline for the common area where participants mingle and munch on snacks prior to the first group meal together. Usually anywhere from one to two dozen people attend, and at the start of a program there's a certain excitement in the air. It's like being a kid on the first day of school, abuzz with curiosity about your classmates and your new homeroom teacher.

It took Tony about five milliseconds to plant himself next to me. The flirtatious vibe was undeniable, but I felt the need for a certain degree of propriety. After all, this *was* a meditation program. Not to make it sound all serious and somber, because that's not what Monroe is like. But it's a mighty strange situation to begin a romance publicly, in the company of close-knit cooped-up strangers.

Tony told the rest of us that he lived in Los Angeles, but I detected his East Coast origins immediately. Instinctively, I responded by launching my Jersey-girl ice-breaking persona, which basically amounts to first class ball-busting. You see, where I come from, if you're too polite, people think you don't like them. Tony joined right in on the fun and readily divulged that Boston had been the scene of his colorful Greek upbringing. But he was currently operating out of Tennessee, making him a sort of Intra-national Man of Mystery.

It's funny how people can be removed from that Right Coast for decades, but if you throw them in a room with other defectors, not only do they instantly recognize each other, but the cultural traditions return with uninterrupted ferocity. In the case of heterosexual courtship, it's more or less the adult verbal version of punching each other on the playground. But then, I suppose you can't have sparks without a little friction.

Cultural compatibility is important, so at this point, Tony was starting to rack up points. My ever-industrious mind was already calculating the prospects for a long-distance relationship. Los Angeles was a mere stone's throw away, and it would take a lot more than an 8-hour drive to drive me away from burgeoning Love. I was putting the cart before the horse, of course, but that's just how my mind operates, coming up with elaborate permutations of any situation. I've learned to roll with it, without putting much weight on the schemings. It's kind of like listening to a child babble on and on and dutifully replying "uh huh... oh...? yes, honey..." The art of self-placation, I guess.

I texted Jolie that night: "I like him :)."

Tony was veritably hilarious, fun-loving and animated, and bursting with positive energy. It turns out he'd been at TMI for one week already, having signed up for three programs back-to-back (which is a completely insane thing to do). As fate would have it, so to speak, a friend of mine had taken the previous week's program with him and later described Tony, rather adeptly, as being "effusive with love from the very beginning." (Another interesting synchronicity: we would later discover that a couple I know were there with Tony for his third week, after I left.) They say it's no accident who shows up for these TMI programs together. Then again, are there ever really "accidents"?

As for the rest of our Guidelines "family," they were all perfectly lovely people, but as the hours and days transpired, I found it increasingly difficult to allocate my time in getting to know any of them. That's because one man began to eclipse all other options. Tony and I gravitated to each other—organically converging in hallways, sitting together purposefully at meals. We unabashedly sought each other out during break times, during which he would smoke and drink coffee out on the deck while I indulged in handfuls of chocolate from the snack table. Already we had become partners in hedonistic crime. Which is only fitting for a Greek guy and an Abraham-Hicks fan-girl.

Deep conversations ensued—about cosmology and consciousness and whatnot—but mainly we just laughed a lot, slipping spontaneously and outrageously into accents and characters, citing obscure vintage cartoons or heavy metal song lyrics with equal ease. He and I had been studying a lot of the same metaphysical teachings, and it seemed our respective grey matter had been imprinted with the same 1970s American pop-culture branding iron.

In many ways, I was looking at a male version of myself, amazed that there could be such a freak. On top of all that compatibility, he was damn cute, and charming too. It was all very swoontastic, especially in the magical firmament of the Monroe Institute.

When I told him I'd had a private question-and-answer session with Bashar—one of his favorite teachers—he literally fell on the ground. (He's a bit dramatic, but it's part of what makes him so fun.) He went ape-shit over the DVD of the session—the one I just *happened* to have with me. I'd tucked it in my bag at the last minute, thinking I was going to share it with Jolie, but she wasn't particularly interested. Apparently it was another one of those clever machinations of the Universe. Between our Bashar connection, and the next morning's incident, Tony was clearly becoming smitten himself.

Normally in TMI programs, there is a yoga class before breakfast, and exercise is strongly encouraged for participants to stay grounded. But it's my custom to skip it and do my own thing, having tried yoga many times to my great dissatisfaction. For me, yoga is a four-letter word. But our Guidelines trainer had informed us there would be Tai Chi... or Qi Gong—he couldn't remember which. So I decided to check it out. I joined the other early-risers in the basement studio and positioned next to me, looking awfully cute in his old-school sweats and bandanna, was Tony.

The instructor arrived—the same one who teaches yoga —and she quickly set things straight. It was, in fact, a yoga class, and our trainer must have been enjoying a senior moment, because it's always been yoga and nothing but.

With that news, I promptly got up and left the room and headed upstairs to re-enact my old Plan A of stretching and exercising on my own. I was surprised when Tony got up and followed me, apparently seizing his opportunity for a semi-graceful exit. It turns out he doesn't like yoga either, and later confessed that my willful rebelliousness was what endeared me to him. Finally, someone who appreciates my finer qualities.

He joined me for some stretching, asking for advice on his tight hamstrings—an overt ploy if ever there was one. *Yes, of course I can help you with that darlin'.* There I was, lying on the plush white carpet next to this happy hunk of a Man, doing some half-assed exercise, but mostly becoming deeply mesmerized by his big blue eyes and long eyelashes as I listened to interesting snippets from his life experience.

I had to admit that Jolie had been right. I was infatuated to say the least, and the prospects were looking good.

♥

Another day of witty banter, riveting conversation and growing energetic connection came to pass. Our Guidelines group of 24 met several times a day, before and after the hemi-sync exercises to prepare and debrief, and increasingly I found Tony stationed nearby. A magnetic field was growing, around and between us. I was feeling more than a little distracted from the program, and a tiny bit anxious.

I decided to use some of the open-ended exercises to ask for guidance about this Man-situation. And why not? The program is all about guidance, but what you apply it to is your own business. To my "inner self helper" I posed the following question: *What is the deal with me and this man?*

My answer came in song form, which is not uncommon for me. Sometimes information is visual, sometimes claircognizant (sudden downloads of knowing). At other times, messages are conveyed through direct experience, metaphoric or otherwise. Whatever the format, when the response arrives lightning-fast, I give it more credence and entertain less skepticism that my conscious mind is making the shit up. So, when I asked that question and immediately heard Gladys Knight singing "take me in your arms and love me," my giddiness got another dose of giddyup.

In the next round of hemi-sync fun, I had another unstructured opportunity for personal guidance, and essentially asked the same question. (I can just imagine my spirit-guides rolling their eyes at my distrust.) This time, it was Sean Hayes, an indie musician I dig, serenading me in reply. His lilting, gorgeous ballad, *"When We Fall In,"* played

31

in my mind's-ear as crisply and accurately as a digital recording on the finest equipment. The lyrics go like this:

> *I am in deep with you darling*
> *I am in deep with you darling*
> *The falling that is ours to enjoy*
> *The opening that is ours to explore*
> *Go on, come on, go on*
> *Let's fall in*
> *I am in deep with you darling*
> *I am in deep with you darling...*
> *I'm your man, I'm your man!*

I'd have to be pretty dense to miss the message in that one. Higher guidance isn't necessarily cryptic.

That afternoon, Tony and I had planned to take a little country stroll during our afternoon break. While I waited for him to meet me in the TMI library, I pulled out my iPod because I wanted to hear that Sean Hayes song again. I was so lost in the music that when I reopened my eyes, it startled me to find Tony standing there, smiling back at me. I passed him my headphones, just as I'd do with any music-loving friend.

He listened blithely and when the song ended, casually mentioned that he'd heard that song before. Not because he knew about Sean Hayes (shockingly few people do)—but because he'd actually *heard it during an out-of-body experience* three months prior. Whoa. That is just *crazy*.

I didn't tell him why I'd been inspired to play that particular song, but instead, just kept the awe tucked away inside my jacket as we walked to Lake Miranon, stopping to commune with trees and visit the giant crystal that lives out in the yard. We talked about all manner of things. There was an easy flow of energy, as if we'd already known each other for ages, and never any awkwardness—well, other than the escalating sexual tension.

Other coincidental details piqued my interest. Like the fact that he was assigned to the very same room and bed that I myself occupied during *my* first Monroe program, the Gateway Voyage—the one he had completed the day before I arrived. It turns out that he registered right before I received Maria's exciting email portending romance.

When Tony and I pulled out our cell phones, people stood aghast, as we were probably the last two humans on Earth to own ancient but still-functioning Razr flip phones —his blue and mine pink, as if color-coded by gender.

The next day at lunch, he attempted to cajole me into staying on for Lifeline—the final program in his epic Monroe triad. I considered it, but quickly dismissed the possibility because, among other things, I'd be wasting my money, given how distracted I already was.

Not that I had any regret with regard to Guidelines. I wasn't getting a whole lot of specific guidance from my "inner self-helper" or guides, but that was okay. When I signed up for the program, I anticipated needing input from the wise ones, or the wise part of me. And yet months later, I was repeatedly getting the sense that I was *already* well-connected to guidance on an everyday basis. So my helpers didn't have much to say. It was all an extravagant feint apparently, but I sure wasn't complaining. That's often how Life works: we think we're doing something for one reason, and we realize afterward that we were led there for an entirely different purpose.

Anyway, I interpreted Tony's friendly prodding as an indication that he wanted to spend more time with me. The end of the program was three days away, and I was secretly hatching a plot in which we'd get a hotel room, then he'd take me to the airport the next day—a classic whirlwind romantic send-off. Since he put the vibe out first, I decided to come clean. Half-shyly, I proposed my bold plan while bracing myself for a negative reaction on his part. I'd been so traumatized over the years by men who respond to admissions of affection with fear and evasion, I actually expected him to have some complicated answer that ultimately pointed to "no."

But before I could complete a sentence, he was smiling and accepting my proposal. "Sure, we'll hang out," he said coolly. Clearly, he was not one of those scared little boys. It still felt like he was holding back a little, though. I was mildly confused about the mixed signals, but at least I knew for sure that he was interested. My concentration improved after that.

During the next hemi-sync exercise, I visited with my great grandmother and my grandma (both "dead" by Earth standards, and that's just an inkling of the sort of fun that Monroe programs provide). It was a sweet rendezvous, and I felt completely bathed in love. The three of us were just sitting there holding hands, and I asked them what they thought about this fellow Tony. Both of them beamed back huge smiles. Eventually I bid them adieu and continued my non-physical adventures, encountering Peggy Lee and Erma Bombeck. Somewhere in the middle of it all, Tony appeared. The scene looked a lot like the open field across from the building we currently lay inside of, each of us physically encased in our respective rooms. Very clearly I saw him smiling at me. It was completely unsolicited by me, but obviously not unwelcome.

"How was that last exercise for you?" he asked me over dinner. I gushed about the amazing LoveFest with my female elders, and the great conversations with famous people... then I suddenly recalled how he had popped in. He started grinning, and explained that he had deliberately "visited me" with the intention of astral sex, knowing how much it meant to me. He chose to focus on that field across the street, because it's where we had been standing and enjoying the scenery earlier that day when I'd brought up the subject.

Wow. I was blown away. What I experienced wasn't quite astral sex, but it was an enormously promising start. To say that this was a dream come true sounds so cliché, but what can I say? I'd finally met a man capable of and interested in multi-dimensional exploration—something I barely thought was possible—and he also happened to be a man to whom I was insanely attracted. My head was spinning. And my heart was bursting with the twitterpation of unprecedented joy. Things would only get better from there.

On our afternoon walk the next day, he commandeered a big umbrella and offered me his arm, "courting" in that old-fashioned way, as he put it. When I hopped over a rickety fence, he was there to brace me. There's nothing like chivalry to sweep a girl off her feet. In the buffet line, he would hand me a plate first, before grabbing his own. His built-in radar was programmed for detecting my needs, and I felt like a Princess in the presence of this sweet Virgo boy. He was quite the gentlemen too, for we hadn't even kissed.

The more I learned, the more lost-in-love I became. I started having all these flashbacks to old boyfriends and different scenes from my Past. This man was a grand culmination of all the Man-excellence I'd encountered firsthand—plus all the other good stuff I longed for but never quite believed was possible.

My text update to Jolie: "I'm in Love! And I'm sorry but I won't be seeing you again before I leave town." Of course she understood. She was hootin' and hollerin' so loud I could almost hear her coming through the electrons in the text message.

♥

In the evenings at these Monroe programs, they often have events and activities other than hemi-sync exercises, just to mix it up—and probably to avoid overload. One night there was a guest speaker, but it was the same guest speaker who'd come to Tony's Gateway program the week before (and mine two years prior). Fascinating as the speaker was, he would probably be re-telling the same stories, so Tony and I decided to skip it—and have the building to ourselves.

I suggested we use some of our free time for the energy healing I'd offered him, and perhaps I could teach him a few dance steps as well. "I'm feeling really inspired to learn how to dance now..." he murmured, evidently *hip*notized by my salsa lessons. The energy work entranced him too, as he could readily feel its effects, being the sensitive tuned-in type of guy that he is.

We took turns playing iPod DJ, relishing the discovery of overlapping turf in our eclectic musical spheres. Our little private party was interrupted when the group started filtering in after the talk, but we relocated to his room where, miraculously, he had not been assigned a roommate. We stayed up late, just talking. When sleep finally won out, I tiptoed back to my own room for a few hours of shut-eye.

The next day, Nicole flashed me a mischievous smile. Tony had garnered her stamp of approval, but she cautioned me briefly, as any good friend would. It's always good to check in with the voice of reason. And usually with me, caution goes unheeded, but this time it was unneeded. Her stance quickly shifted to one of co-creative excitement.

Then came Movie Night. They showed a great '80s flick, *Made in Heaven*. I got inspired to gather up some pillows and blankets, and camp out on the floor, rather than be confined to the conference room chairs. Seamlessly, Tony and I snapped into team mode to implement my brilliant plan.

Before long we were getting pretty snuggly (finally... some tactile satisfaction!) though nothing crazy, mind you, because we were right up front in the room. After the movie, Tony had the even cleverer idea to take our cozy nest-makings up to the rooftop observation deck.

It was an exceedingly cold, clear night in a week of clouded-over skies. So very many stars! I suppose my extremities were becoming numb—if I'd cared to notice. I was lying with a beautiful man and the entire galaxy was looking back at me, winking and twinkling and shooting off its celestial fireworks. My internal effervescence mirrored the scene above, and I could barely stop giggling. Soon he was kissing me, and it was even better than I imagined. All that built-up tension was suddenly, mutually unleashed. I've always been a fan of instant gratification, but for the first time, I understood the beauty of the wait. Things started getting hot and heavy, so we relocated to his room, and... well, I'm not one to get too graphic, so I'll just say we probably had more fun in that little room than all the previous occupants combined. Then again, ours wasn't the first Monromance to happen under that roof, and it won't be the last. Oh, if only those walls could speak.

We eventually fell asleep, nestled together in the cozy enclosed twin bed until the morning affirmation played over the speakers, narrated by Bob Monroe, "our granpappy" as we like to call him.

The next day I wondered whether Tony would shun me or be publicly affectionate, as I was *still* coming from that battle-weary place of historical relationship dysfunction. So I braced myself for unpreferred scenarios, but that proved to be unnecessary and downright silly. This was a Man with strength of character, and his ability to know himself and communicate his feelings would continue to bowl me over. Ah, one more fear assuaged and taken out of production.

At the program's end, we said our goodbyes and made our way to the Doubletree Hotel. Alone, together—at last. And with a king-sized bed, which seemed oceanic. The sexual chemistry was so off-the-hook, I joked that we'd both just gotten out of jail. We squeezed a lot of living into our final 24 hours together. Plus the chivalry continued: he took me out on a proper date with dinner and wine, opened doors for me and picked up the bill.

We had so readily taken on that *couple* energy, calling each other pet names and happily accommodating each other's needs. It felt just like a honeymoon. Everything about our relationship seemed accelerated and condensed, as if we were in "review mode" from other lifetimes, eager to get up to speed and get busy writing the next chapter.

There was, however, a brief somber moment that interrupted the fun. It was when he pulled away emotionally, and though it came in an innocent-sounding comment, I was on to him. I let it upset me for a little while before agreeing to brush it aside. The party must go on— especially with few precious hours left on the clock. When it was time to head to the airport, he carried my bags, and we stopped for coffee en route. In the terminal, we asked idle passengers to take our picture, leaving no space for melancholy in our remaining minutes.

Who knew when we'd meet again, or where? It was all very nebulous. But I felt perfectly bubbly as I boarded my plane, wired and tired from sleep deprivation and the Starbucks sleep-replacer coursing through my veins. A new friend who had been in the Guidelines program shared the first leg of my itinerary, so he and I sat together and chatted the flight away, which steered my mind far from mournful sighing, if I would be so inclined. Which I wasn't. I was riding the momentum of the Love High as far as I could.

Tony, on the other hand, was left on the ground, feeling the sharp pangs of separation—a switch from his detached happy-go-lucky front the night before. He returned to the Monroe Institute for the Lifeline program, but ironically, found the place relatively lifeless without me. It would be another three weeks before he realized that he, too, was in Love. Women are usually quicker on the draw when it comes to matters of the heart.

He had been assuming it was just a fling, and that he'd be plugging back into his previously scheduled life plans upon leaving TMI: launching his business in Tennessee, then returning to Los Angeles four to six months later. The only problem with his scheme was that it was hatched by his logical, calculating, Earthbound mind. His higher mind, apparently, was cooking up some *different* plans.

I returned to San Francisco, lovestruck, giddily sleep-deprived, and uncompromisingly optimistic. After floating home, I pulled out the Man-list I'd created months earlier, and marveled at the precision with which Tony's qualities mirrored my specifications. Smart, cute, sweet and super fun? Check. Likes traveling, hiking, music? Check. Cooks, cleans, dances, and gives massages? Check. Sexual dynamo? Check. Open-minded and woo-woo, but not *too* woo-woo? Check…double check. *Well played, Universe.*

Love Story to be continued...

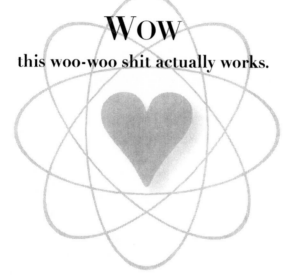

WOW
this woo-woo shit actually works.

"Mind is the master weaver, both of the inner garment of character and the outer garment of circumstance."
—James Allen

If you understand that your thoughts create reality, and you know what sorts of realities you prefer, then why is this so hard? I mean, why aren't you basking in the goods already? Has something gone terribly wrong? Well, yes and no. There definitely *is* a hitch at the git-along, cowgirl, but it's not so terrible. You can lasso it to the ground any time.

I'm going to offer you a helpful construct. Imagine that the mind—your mind, my mind, anyone's mind—is really a set of conjoined twins named Physical Mind and Higher Mind. Physical Mind is "down here" in the trenches of physical reality, focused in the direct sensory experience of life as a human. She often gets so absorbed in The Drama

© 2013 Anthony Scarpelos

that she forgets she even *has* a twin. Higher Mind, however, never loses sight of her twin. They are, after all, inseparable. It's just that Physical Mind can have the *experience* of being alone and separate. These twins may *appear* to dwell in distinctly different realms, but that too is just a perspective, an illusion. It's all part of the ingenious game they're playing.

The game is akin to a multi-dimensional team version of chess, with Physical Mind stationed on the valley floor and Higher Mind up on the

42

mountaintop. H-mind, from this unlimited vantage point, is able to offer instruction to her twin: "go left, do a backflip, stay put for a moment... now move forward." P-mind does well to heed her twin's advice, since she herself cannot see beyond her immediate surroundings. It's important to note that each twin needs the other in order to play this Life-on-Earth game, and together they form a complete holistic being. Cooperation and specialization of labor makes for a well-oiled machine—a winning team, if you will.

The game's overall objective, though, is merely to be in it. The experience itself is valued, rather than the achievement of any particular goals. That said, conjuring and realizing goals along the way is just part of the experience. There are no points, no finish lines, no competition with other teams. Higher Mind remains eternally patient, tireless, loving, and supportive, no matter what happens. Physical Mind, on the other hand, has a more emotionally erratic experience playing the game, due to the nature of her position.

Here is another way to construe their relationship. Imagine these twins are traveling in a car, with H-mind behind the wheel, and P-mind in the back, *facing backward* (like an antique car's rumble seat or the "way-back" seat of a big ol' 1970s station wagon). P-mind is very good at using her five senses and her powers of reasoning to detect all the goings-on around her, and she assigns meaning to whatever she perceives. But she only has access to the Present and the Past of her experience. She's literally in no position to see the road ahead. The good news is, she doesn't *need* to, as H-mind is a most excellent, skilled and thoughtful chauffeur.

P-mind often has a destination she fancies, and she frequently comes up with new requests for her driver. H-mind is happy to oblige. Like a savvy New Yorker in a cab, Physical Mind may attempt to dictate the route. But unlike that New Yorker, P-mind is not very savvy and knows but a few of the infinite options for getting there, so her instructions are more of a hindrance than a help. That's because she's not actually *capable* of hatching a masterful plan — she can only recycle old experiences that she's already observed, then project those onto a Future timeframe. Physical Mind simply lacks access to the full set of data.

Higher Mind, however, *does* have the scoop. Left unfettered, H-mind selects a route that provides the best possible experiences — say, winding by an exquisite new-to-you ice cream parlor, or crossing the path of an old friend or the stranger who will be hiring you for your awesome new job. H-mind effortlessly delivers a *version* of the requested "destination" that's fabulous beyond your wildest schemes.

Nonetheless, P-mind often chooses to forsake H-mind's considerable wisdom, insisting that *she knows* what's best. In that case, H-mind simply behaves like a GPS unit and continually recalculates the route. P-mind may become distinctly unhappy with her experience along such "inferior" routes of her own devising. The illusion of disconnection from her twin begets fear, worry and anger, so things may get a little tense in their "vehicle of consciousness" whenever P-mind is immersed in The Drama. Still, Higher Mind remains the ever-complicit servant, steering the car to safety as best she can, no matter how many tantrums Physical Mind chooses to throw. They'll arrive at some version of the destination sooner or later. But the road trip is so much more delightful when each twin gets to do the job she's actually cut out to do.

Now, in case you're tempted to infer that Physical Mind is somehow lessor or junior to Higher Mind, I have one more analogy that might help balance things out. Think of H-mind as an air traffic controller and P-mind as the pilot.

Both are absolutely indispensable; they simply have different skill sets and perspectives. The system works well when Pilot P-mind puts her trust in H-mind ground control. Physical Mind knows that she's headed to Denver, for instance, but concerns herself only with the immediate indicators. She allows Higher Mind to guide her as she goes, changing course and elevation as needed to avoid collisions and make the trip more fun and efficient.

It's a brilliantly designed game to be sure, but many people experience hijackings that leave H-mind bound and gagged while the unlicensed, myopic P-mind (wo)mans the controls. Who's the terrorist? The ego-intellect—that know-it-all who's really just a scaredy-cat underneath. And who is, ironically, just trying to *protect you* from uncomfortable emotions, even as it generates them.

Attempting to predict and manage the Future details of your life experience purely from the logical Physical Mind can make you crazy—*and* stave off the mating season. *But we can fix this.* And it will come as a great relief because frankly, P-mind's dysfunction is exhausting. Let go. Relax. *Trust.* Okay, I understand that might be easier said than done, but it doesn't need to happen all at once. Just begin by *considering* the idea of loosening the reins a bit more.

You don't actually have to *believe* you're being driven to a unicorns-and-lollypops wonderland where your Prince awaits along with everything else you desire. You don't even have to *believe* that the Man of Your Dreams exists. You need not *believe* much of anything if you can learn to stop *actively disbelieving*. Vacillating between belief and disbelief is very common, but the key to riding that wave, as you'll soon see, is forming new patterns of *non-interference*.

Fortunately, Higher Mind is exceedingly clever and unrelenting in getting through to stubborn Physical Mind.

Guidance arrives in a multitude of ways: a bumper sticker in front of you with an undeniably relevant message; a sudden overwhelming urge to do something; a recurrent dream; a novel thought that pops in your head unrelated to preceding mental chatter; or perhaps the old voices-in-the-head gag.

FUNdamental Truth #1

YOU DON'T NEED TO BELIEVE…
AS LONG AS YOU STOP ACTIVELY DISBELIEVING.

Regardless of the delivery method, your Higher Mind *will* leave you a trail of popcorn. It's been happening all along, even if you've been unaware, trampling it underfoot. It may only be one kernel at a time, but that's all you really need. Not that the "you" reading this is pure Physical Mind, because we're complex multi-dimensional critters, but just to keep things simple, I refer to "you" as the physical being who's here seeing, hearing, touching, tasting, smelling, and also planning, scheming, plotting, *meddling, fretting…*

Specialization of "Labor"

YOUR JOB ➡	WHAT WHY	What do you really want? Why do you want it?
NOT YOUR JOB ➡	HOW WHO WHEN WHERE	Be joyfully curious, but unconcerned, about the MANifestation details, including timing. Allow Higher Mind to drive.

Hey, you just dropped 2/3 of the work. Don't you feel lighter?

The Cosmic Café

"The personal world we each live in, with all of its unique characters, friends, loved ones, dramas, challenges, joys and sorrows, is a direct reflection of our inner mental and emotional states of mind. If you want to alter the outer scenario, you must learn how to alter the inner one."
—Rick Stack

Hungry for some good lovin'? Alright, then pull up a chair, and let's get started. We are all essentially customers, forever seated in an etheric restaurant—ordering and being served, over and over and over again. Unceasingly, we're also sifting through the offerings, declaring some tasty and others vile. Our order-placing happens effortlessly and without fanfare, because the Cosmic Waitress is telempathic—meaning, she picks up on our thoughts *and* our feelings.

We're constantly emitting signals from our minds, and the Cosmic Waitress is standing by, jotting it all down. She never tires, slacks off, or cops an attitude. She's like a benevolent robot at your service, recording your every dictation without fail, and without judgment. She always captures the essence of what you're focused on—and if you focus on it often enough and with enough feeling, she has the Cosmic Kitchen staff bring it to your table.

So, what's on your plate right now? If you're staring at some unpalatable gruel, I know it must be mighty annoying to hear me say that you ordered it. Well, it's perfectly okay if you can't recall requesting that wretched bowl of slumgullion. We'll just say you were drunk when you slung the menu around. But don't you worry because there's time enough to dry up and get yourself a proper meal.

The Cosmic Waitress is equivalent to the classic uncorked genie who has only one thing to say: *"Your wish is my command."* But "wishes" can be made unconsciously and to your chagrin, because anything you think about often enough is going to show up in your experience, whether or not you *wish* it would.

© 2013 Anthony Scarpelos

Immersed in our Life experience, we encounter a mind-bogglingly diverse array of situations, and naturally we enjoy some more than others. Our thoughts about these life scenes, and our ensuing *emotional responses to those thoughts*, are not "forgotten" by the Universe—even if they quickly vanish from our personal conscious awareness. That means the Cosmic Waitress still has a notation about how much you adored (okay, stalked) David Cassidy when you were twelve, and a rendezvous with Mr. Cassidy could, theoretically, be arranged at any time. Sure, the likelihood is low, but only because the idea has not been *active* in your vibration for a very long time.

There is never a time when we stop ordering, and Gluttony-of-Experience *is* the ultimate driving force of the Universe. It is a ceaseless natural process. Even if you're meditating with a blank peaceful mind (and good luck with that), you're still requesting "more blank peace, please" because the orders are generated by your mind-pictures, ideas and feelings, rather than just words. Every moment is a string of new micro-manifestations, and in each moment, a new set of orders is placed and processed. The resulting manifestations may not *seem* new to us when their differences are imperceptibly slight—and that's because we keep repeating the same old orders on auto-pilot.

When you're having a sucky time playing the Earth game, you are still identifying desires and preferences in that moment—namely, the opposite of whatever is sucking. When this happens, you're emitting dueling signals (cue the banjo music). So which one will you experience more of, *the preferred or the unpreferred?* Which dish comes out of the Cosmic Kitchen first or is served to you on a bigger platter? The answer is straightforward: whichever one you devote more energy to.

Obviously there's a helluva lot of ordering going on in this all-night empyrean diner. Not *every* stray thought materializes in some big bold obvious way—and thank god for that. A certain critical mass is required. It's as if the Waitress is asking *"are you sure, hon?"* before actually submitting your order to the Cosmic Kitchen. Our most commonly held thought-sequences and scenarios, particularly the ones involving strong emotional responses, are the ones that stand out on the Cosmic Chef's list of priorities. It's kind of like Twitter or Facebook—the most recent and/or popular "mind-posts" garner more attention. Which is a real boon when you think about it, because that means you can turn your wayward ship around relatively quickly with a powerful blast of *preferred* thinking.

By the way, is it slightly embarrassing to think that "someone" is tracking your every mental-move? Well, the truth is, your mind is naked before the Universe. There can be no secrets in the Cosmic Café, so you might as well relax and come clean. You couldn't lose your Cosmic Waitress if you wanted to. You'd be like a two-year-old playing hide-and-seek by covering her own eyes—cute, but not exactly efficacious.

Anyway, I'm quite sure you signed up to play a game that's far more challenging and rewarding than hide-and-seek. It's the grown-up human wizardry game of "decide what you want, then allow it to unfold." You're more than qualified; you just need to brush up on the rulebook. Ready to take the controls off auto-pilot?

Order Up!

"You are knowing what you are wanting, yes?"
—Abraham-Hicks

List-making is certainly a favorite activity for the single woo-woo gal. We love scribing fancy handmade paper with special purple pens, cataloguing important man-qualities and adorning it with hearts, sparkles, smileys, and infinity symbols, then placing the list in some special Feng Shui vessel where it co-habitates with rose petals, rose quartz crystals and other man-wheedling talismen. Perhaps we'll burn a sacred scroll in a solstice ritual, asking that the pagan gods of romance carry asunder the ashes, returning them to us in the form of a fully materialized man-mate. Or maybe we just scribble some shit on a cocktail napkin after a few salty rounds of margaritas. Or log it neatly in a geeky love-spreadsheet.

Whether you spray-paint it on a pole or shout it from the mountaintops, your list is *not* created for the purpose of letting the Universal Santa know what you want for Christmas. That communication happens automatically, and everything that's important to you in a relationship, thus far, has been noted.

Your list *does* provide clarity and focus, which are essential for morale now, and for discernment later on. Rather than simply respond to what's currently available, you need to be proactive in specifying what you want, even if you don't currently see it stocked on the shelves of the Man-store. This is also the case for seeking a new job or home or anything that's important to you. Don't just settle for "what-is."

What do you *really* want and *why* do you want it? Exploring the answers in-depth will serve you in a multitude of ways, but for starters, it sparks your appetite. Your "Men-U" is virtually unlimited—anything you can dream up, the Cosmic Kitchen can whip up. So, what is it that you're craving?

In her cute little book, *If the Buddha Dated*, Charlotte Kasl defines nine levels of interaction, from the physical through the spiritual. The structured exercises, combined with her gentle verbiage, prompt you to think long and deep about what you're looking for in a relationship, possibly in ways you haven't considered before. I highly recommend checking it out.

This Man-list task should be deliriously fun. If it isn't, then you're clearly not in the right frame of mind, and you should switch to a different subject or activity until you're feeling sufficiently groovy. You're going to hear me talk a lot about the significance of emotions and becoming finely tuned to them. I may even begin to sound like a broken record, but it's just too important to risk glossing over. This is an emotional journey we're on. It's not the tired old story of denial and reproach, but rather, a newfound understanding and optimization of our emotional gifts as kick-ass tools for happiness.

When you're feeling reasonably happy, brainstorming your ideal guy gets you in the vibrational mood (heh heh). But the same process, when you're feeling crappy, leads to unnecessary, unhelpful limitation. Make it your goal to simply *become more aware* of wherever you're currently perched on the emotional spectrum.

The better your mood, the more objective you can be, especially if you're investigating *why* you want what you want. Will the Man of Your Dreams provide opportunities for you to express love, share your experience, and get some action on a regular basis? Or are you seeking someone to take care of you, or "make you" feel better about yourself? That is some potentially deep shit, and you'll be better equipped for honest self-assessment when you're *not* in the middle of an emotional maelstrom.

Here's a powerful idea for list-making: list not just *his* qualities, but also what *you* bring to the table. Often we remain fixated on what we want to *receive* and forget to "advertise" what it is we're *offering*. It helps fortify your self-esteem. If your lovely Waitress is moonlighting as a Cosmic Matchmaker, why not slip her your credentials?

Your Man *is* definitely out there and will eventually home in on your signals like a cartoon bear to a fresh-baked blueberry pie. It's like this. You improvise his Woman-list and the Law of Attraction locates the man whose preferences match your qualities. Get as specific and creative as you can. Plus it's going to be a lot of fun when the two of you meet up and compare notes.

That brings us to this zestful slice of Universal truth: *what you seek is also seeking you*. There are no one-sided coins in this world; for every Frick there's a Frack. Hey, look, that's just Life in Duality—I'm not making this shit up. As one of my favorite teachers, Lisa French, explains: "when you have a dream, there *has* to be someone out there who shares that same dream."

Your Dreamboat will be every bit as psyched to have *you* in his life as you will be to have him. You don't need to believe that right now, but do take note of the valuable information your reaction provides. Maybe you're like I was, feeling doubtful that my specifications could be met. But then again, you might be in another camp—the one where you're not quite sure that you're *worthy* of Mr. Awesome.

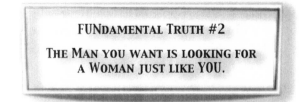

Your Man-list is a springboard for visualization. It's your reminder to focus your thought ray-gun on the desired target. Visualizing doesn't need to be literally visual, but just some form of imagining things the way you'd ideally love them to be. Did you ever get reprimanded as a child for daydreaming too much? Excellent. That propensity serves you well.

Imagination, in the service of good vibes, is your best friend, and it can take you to magnificent places. But when the mind gets hijacked, imagination easily devolves into a terrorist and creates scenarios of precisely what you *don't* want. So, again, *the way you feel* — when visualizing, when creating your Man-list, and whenever you're thinking about the subject or doing anything else that's important to your goals — will determine your results. Make a policy of doing your deliberate imagining *only* when you're in a good mood. Otherwise, just change the channel.

There are things about Tony that initially seemed like bonus goodies thrown in by the Universe because I hadn't included them specifically on my Man-list. I say "initially," because once I realized that the order-placing step is truly automated, it became obvious to me that the list contents aren't all that important.

Tony's love of cats was one of those "bonus" items. I didn't deliberately add this to my list because my Physical Mind told me it wasn't possible. Well, I had hard evidence, you know — from my keen observations of the Past. Up until that point, most of the men I'd been attracted to were dog-lovers, and lukewarm, at best, about kitties. While that was statistically true of my Past, projecting it onto my Future reality was unnecessarily limiting. It was a breach of contract between P-mind and H-mind.

After some intensive study of the Law of Attraction, I stopped reinforcing those old limiting thoughts, and in doing so I became receptive to what I truly desired: a man who loves both cats and dogs (and everyone else). Note that I didn't need to focus on a new positive replacement thought, such as "many attractive single men love cats." The Waitress already recorded the fact that I loved cats and cat lovers, from a lifetime of experiences, so *dropping the naysayer routine was all that was required.*

Ladies, I cannot stress this enough: Do not allow your orders to be curtailed by "what-is-itis"!

Far greater possibilities exist than you can currently perceive or even imagine. That's because the portion of reality (yes, it is but a mere portion) that any of us has access to at any given moment hinges on our personal unconscious belief systems, as well as our current vibrational state. If you find yourself saying things like "oh, that's not realistic," nip it in the bud. There is no need to envision the big picture of your MANifestation with all its minutiae—and you never can do that anyway, until it's right in front of your face—but you *do* need to quit raining on your own parade.

Here's an example of what *not* to do. Years ago, I often felt depressed and pessimistic about my dating prospects and a lot of other things. My foul mood resulted in a considerably diminished wish-list. I recall specifying, in a particularly pitiful moment, "someone to love... and I don't even care if he's monogamous or not." Well, what do you suppose happened? The next time I got into a long-range romantic entanglement, the most contentious issue between us was his ambivalence about monogamy. In truth, I'm all about monogamy, but my depressed state had made it possible for me to lie to myself and deny my true desires. You deserve so much more than what a constrictive, low-vibratory mood has to offer.

MAN POINTER #1

ONLY DO YOUR DELIBERATE ORDERING WHEN YOU'RE IN A GOOD MOOD.

Conversely, in my more recent, jubilant days, the qualifications I focused on prior to meeting Tony were quite extensive. Somewhere on the third page I'd written "he likes to read to me"—a small but very particular request. It turns out this is one of his favorite things. During our long distance courtship, he read to me every night over the phone, and ever since, we've continued the custom of reading books together almost daily. While reading aloud may not be everyone's idea of a good time, it goes to show that *specificity is on your side…* but *only* if you're in the requisite frame of mind to do the specifying. Ya dig?

You'll recall that Higher Mind can conceive of infinite delightful solutions to any request, while Physical Mind can only look back and perceive what's already been done. Does the Man of Your Dreams exist in your Past? Probably not. Or at least, not entirely. For this reason, it's a good idea to emphasize—in your mind and on your collage or list as a reminder—the classic statement that *"this or something better"* is now lining up in the Universe, for the highest good of all concerned. That last clause is also key, because it reminds you that you're not taking away from anyone else's happiness in getting what *you* want. It's win-win, all around.

You might think of it this way: everything you've ever wanted already exists in a vibrational format, or "in the vortex" as they say, and your strong desire for those things means you are psychically peeking into that vortex. So you don't need to concern yourself with any "sins of omission" from your orders. Your demeanor is a gazillion times more important than making sure you've crossed every "t" and dotted every "i" on your Man-list, so stay away from topics that throw you for a loop—unless or until you're ready to transcend them. It's okay to leave them out of the equation entirely—the Cosmic Waitress has got your back.

If, at any point, you find yourself in some crappy emotional terrain, here's your psychological first aid kit: decide that it's *okay* to be wherever you are. We all go there from time to time—it's just part of the human experience. No big whoop. Your best bet is to do something that makes you feel better, which might just be taking a nap. Or a walk. Or whatever works for *you*.

If you're up for it, you might venture to move up through the emotional continuum by reaching for less-specific, more-general thoughts on the current subject. Let's say you're stuck on a rant like this: "Another broke guy, too cheap to pay. All these guys are losers! They can't even spring for a pizza. I'm surrounded by cheapskates who are out of work and want me to pay for everything..." You can select more *general, but still negative*, thoughts such as: "well, maybe they're not *all* broke—after all, they could be losers in some other way. Lots of things are possible. And I haven't met *every* single man in this town yet."

The idea is to take baby steps in accordance with your emotional state. You're not in a rush to get anywhere—

you're simply striving to feel better. Did you know that anger is actually a step up from feeling depressed and disempowered? If you drop the self-judgment about being wherever you're at, it'll be easier to move on up.

Then, when you're in a brighter mood, you can opt for *generally positive* thoughts such as: "there are lots of possibilities and lots of wonderful men in the world." Ultimately, when you're feeling exuberant, you'll have access to *specifically positive* thoughts on the same topic, like: "there are men who are generous, well-off, and who love treating their woman to nice meals, and my Man is one of them!" When it comes to certain issues, you might not ever get there to *specific and positive*, but there's absolutely nothing wrong with that. It's just like my example of cat-loving men. Whatever the subject is, either get behind it or get out of the way — by first assessing what you're capable of emotionally.

Emotional guidance is a profoundly useful tool once you've read and understood the operating manual. The Abraham-Hicks teachings have been hugely illuminating for me and thousands of others. They're surprisingly practical, and often humorous too. You build a better vibration, bit by bit, neutralizing negativity, just like shifting a car's transmission into Neutral before changing direction. You can't really go directly from first gear to fifth, right? Easy does it.

Since I'm a do-it-yourself artsy kind of gal, I made a big collage to remind myself of my personal "no loitering in low vibratory places" policy. (It's on my website in case you'd like to see or download a larger, full-color version.)

Okay, so, back to the list-making merriment. Besides creating lists of individual traits (yours and his), you could also make lists or dialogues that describe how the two of

you fit together—what it's like being together, what you guys are doing, saying, feeling. Consider different points of view— yours, his, and even third party observers like friends or family, or strangers who observe you and your Man. A relationship is a two-way street at least, so why not explore every possible love-vector? This builds a more palpable, stalwart vision of your relationship, extending it multi-dimensionally and calling in cooperative components like a big festive astral cocktail party. "Cooperative components," by the way, means any helpful people (co-creators), situations, resources, timing, or what-have-you that play a part in your MANifestation, whether it's a starring role, a bit part or just a cameo.

You might even write a Man-U-Script with lines that you and your Man say to each other. This is powerful stuff, and if you've got an inner playwright, you can really go to town. Even if you don't pride yourself on creative writing, give it a try. Don't worry that you're not skilled enough to craft it or that it's too corny. Give yourself a break from all that criticism.

I scripted some dialogues that ended up being closely mirrored by my interactions with Tony later on. Another woman I know did the Man-U-Scripting (and some other techniques), met the Man of Her Dreams, and was blown away a few weeks later when he was *literally* saying to her the exact words she had scripted. Did I mention that this shit works? Do you have goose bumps yet? Well, you should, because these are true stories, and yours can be added to the collection if you stay on board with this mind-taming work.

Why not create some sort of visual art—a treasure map, vision board, collage, drawing, or some other counterpart to the old-fashioned list? You don't need to define yourself as having artistic talent; anything that gets your right brain involved can be surprisingly helpful. Try molding your thought-energy into some clay. Or food. Or make a recording, if you're partial to audio—like an affirmation stream or a self-hypnotherapy session. Place reminders and love notes around the house. Make up songs or poems if that's fun. Do an interpretive dance. Stage a puppet show… I dunno, whatever floats your boat.

Whatever you do, make it your priority to pay attention to your emotional state. If gazing at your vision board every day energizes you, then prominently displaying it is a fine idea. But if you feel a tinge of hopelessness when it catches your eye, then by all means, put the dang thing away in a drawer.

Things are working out for me.

By the way, about the scripting, I've gotta fill you in on a little more of my personal odyssey. One day in September, when I was working on my first book, I got inspired to do a little creative writing side-project. I called it the Epic-log to the book—an exciting sort of "this just in" redemptive addendum to my woeful romantic history already divulged in several of the chapters. In this fictionalized account, I gurgled that I'd just met the Man of

My Dreams, and was enjoying some other notable manifestations, including the rare car I'd been stalking online. It was fun to write, but I soon filed it away, forgot about it, shared it with no one, and resumed my editing work.

In January, right before my book hit the press, I travelled to the Monroe Institute for the Guidelines program and... well, you know the rest of *that* story. When I re-discovered my Epic-log later on, I think I must have squealed out loud.

The conspicuous moral here is: craft your story as you'd like it to be, and hold nothing back. The more detailed your lists and collages and scripts are, the more fodder you have for visualizing the goods, and the easier it will be to have your order accurately filled the first time. The genie *will* grant your wishes, sooner or later. And you can help it be sooner rather than later, by releasing Resistance (much more on that to come). But let's face it, when it comes to the Man of Your Dreams, wishing is weak. Wishy-washy. To merely wish and hope is to give your power away, but to sincerely *intend* is to claim it. As the great Ernest Holmes once said: "We all need more backbone and less wishbone."

MAN POINTER #2

**HOPING AND WISHING IS WEAK.
INTENTION GETS US THE GOODS.**

A Word (or two thousand) about Being Picky

*"There's only one of us here: what we give to others,
we give to ourselves. What we withhold from others,
we withhold from ourselves."*
—Marianne Williamson

I've been accused of extreme pickiness at times—mostly by myself, but occasionally by others who, I'm sure, meant well. They and I had taken on some not-so-helpful beliefs that if my Man-specifications were too elaborate, then surely I would end up a lonely old maid. Wrong! (Bzzzz... thank you for playing.)

Do you think that wanting the Man of Your Dreams is asking too much? Does it seem greedy or selfish or "unrealistic" to create a long laundry list of man-qualities? Do you sometimes tell yourself that because your life is good enough already, you can't rightly ask for anything more?

Let's get something straight. Romantic Love is *not* in competition with the other parts of your life. Having a nice house, great friends, family, a fun job, or financial success does not make you ineligible for a SupraLove. That's like saying "oh, I already have an arm, so, I don't need a leg." Your various desires are not mutually exclusive, and any limiting assertions to the contrary are the product of definitions and beliefs you acquired along the way. The great news is that you can re-negotiate everything. But you have to know first what you're negotiating with, and what your preferred outcomes are.

Many people operate under the assumption that Life is about achieving goals, and once you "get there," if you're still wanting, then something is wrong with you. And if you never "get there," well, then something is really, *really* wrong.

But I'm here to insist that Life is designed as a process in which we continually identify new desires, come into alignment with them, watch them materialize, then immediately turn around and find more things that we want to have, be, do, and experience. You're never done, and the desire is part of the formula. Why condemn it when you can enjoy it?

You say "picky" like it's a bad thing...

The desire to "merge" with others is a fundamental longing shared by all of humanity. We're all part of the invisible interconnected whole, the One, the only, the all-that-is Source Energy, yet we're focused here playing the individuated-person game. It's such a well-orchestrated illusion that the separation feels very real—and decidedly lonely at times. So, we're always trying to reconnect in some way—whether it's through an online forum, the Ladies Auxiliary, or the corner bar. We unconsciously seek out people who are a lot like us, and who are "outward" representations of our insides.

Specifically, the urge to merge as a pair of equal and opposite genders is a subject treated exhaustively elsewhere, so I won't go there, but suffice it to say that *your desire for a male counterpart* with very specific qualities is anything but unwarranted. It's completely natural and understandable.

Consider this. *Any* person who enters your life, if studied long enough, could be described with a rather lengthy list of attributes, possibly filling numerous volumes with their quirks, history, likes and dislikes, mannerisms, interactions with others, and so on. People are unique and multi-faceted, so there is much to be said about each one of us. Now imagine there is a humongous book that contains detailed profiles for every human being on the planet. If you were to read through this monstrous book, you would *eventually* find the guy that's perfect for you. That would be prohibitively tedious, of course. But my point is that, other than the unlikely case in which he's a one-dimensional cartoon character, your Man is going to have a lot of details.

By specifying a great deal of information about your guy upfront, you are keying in to his particular bio in that big-ass book. You're psychically indexing him, saving yourself a lot of time and hassle from having to read and weed through all the impostors and lookalikes. It's like slipping yourself the answers to an upcoming exam. Why would you *not* want to have that advantage? Do you prefer doing things the hard way?

Placing limitations on your desires is like shooting yourself in the foot. Sure, later on, when MANifestations start knocking on your door, you *may* want to carefully re-assess your lists and weigh your options, but at the ordering stage of the game, absolutely not! So, what on Earth could possess a gal to brandish a weapon and point it ped-ward like that while seeming to defy all logic, reason and self-preservation?

Erroneous beliefs, that's what. We'll go deeper into belief inspection in the Coming Clean section, but right now we need to clear something up: the Cosmic Kitchen functions with zero regard to whether your orders are—according to you or other people—small or large, practical or outlandish, high-maintenance or humble, "realistic" or not. Those are Physical Mind designations. They're unneeded, and they're unwanted.

The very notion of being "too selective" or "too" anything is nothing more than human judgmental mudslinging; far

64

from "factual" information that you must swallow. Culturally, it's born from disgruntled masses over countless generations who felt disempowered and who didn't understand how to work with Universal Law to obtain their desires. Their realities reflected back to them the "solid proof" of their belief systems (as do ours). Underneath it all are the twin myths of scarcity and competition, which are reinforced with common sayings like, "Take what you can get." They're further pummeled into our psyches with religious notions of human inferiority and unworthiness.

FUNDAMENTAL TRUTH #3

YOU CAN NEVER BE TOO PICKY WHEN PLACING YOUR ORDERS IN THE COSMIC CAFÉ.

How many times have you heard someone say, "You can't have your cake and eat it too"? That has got to be the biggest crock of shit in the annals of human history! What is the point of living if you are to be presented with a yummy dessert but forbidden to stick your fork in the thing? Do you honestly believe that Life is intended to be an unsatisfying struggle by design? The gospel truth of our time-space reality is that we absolutely *can* do, be, or have whatever we want, *as long as we decide we're worthy of it.* That decision is ours alone.

I'm going to tell you a little story. A group of ladies, who are mostly single, work together in an office. One of them, Terri, is considered by her co-workers to be difficult and selfish. She's notorious for maximizing her personal gain with blatant disregard to other people's needs or opinions. She's a "looking out for number one" kind of gal.

Now, Terri knows about the Law of Attraction—both instinctively, and from perusing New Age reading materials. She set out to land herself a Man, and she knew exactly what she wanted. Her co-workers knew too, because Terri wasn't shy about divulging her intentions. A month later, Terri met her Man: the perfect match to her list of preferred credentials. Her co-workers were impressed with the MANifesting, but equally annoyed that Terri got what she wanted. "It's not fair!" they complained, that such a selfish woman should have such a wonderful man as him.

News flash: *The Universe doesn't care what you think is or isn't fair.* Well, it's not that "it" doesn't care for you, because of course the Universe is all about unconditional love and support. Hell, it'll even back you up when you insist you're not worthy of the Man of Your Dreams. Your wish is its command, no matter what. The Universe does not engage in moral judgments of any kind. Only humans do this.

Terri is actually a great teacher because she exemplifies the cut-and-dried nature of Universal Law. She got what she wanted because she was clear about her desires, felt she deserved them (or him, in this case), and put up virtually no Resistance. She did not judge herself, nor did she allow herself to become adversely affected by the judgments of others. In short, she emanated a relatively *unconflicted vibration.* And the Universe, which operates unerringly on physics and not favoritism, was compelled to mechanically drop the goods in her lap.

I'm not saying we should idolize Terri. Duh. Though I'm sure she has admirable qualities just as anyone does, I'm primarily suggesting that there is great value in transcending judgmentality. Not to be pious, because that's just another kind of judgment, but because it *feels good.* If you've been acting like Terri's co-workers, chances are you're prone to

66

judging *yourself*; if you think Terri is not entitled to a SupraLove, maybe you don't actually think you're worthy of one either. It's that pesky mirroring thing.

If you're feeling jealous or resentful of another woman who's got her man, you've probably got an "I believe in scarcity and competition" program running in the background. Some women actually think, "Oh great, there's another one taken off the market..." when a quality dude gets scooped up by his new lady-friend. These sorts of thoughts do not serve you. It's just another case of ego-hijacking. If this is you, don't fret, darlin'. You have the power to tell a new story... and the choice to laugh about it, rather than scold yourself.

When the Cosmic Waitress brings out your very own tasty Man-dish, you don't want to miss out because you're too busy nosing around in other people's dishes. Nor do you want your dish to get cold while you're over at the wrong table with Mr. Appetizer and your back turned to the Waitress... but we'll get to that subject a little later.

FUNDAMENTAL TRUTH #4

KNOWING AND FEELING THAT YOU DESERVE YOUR DESIRES IS A GREEN LIGHT TO THE UNIVERSE.

Look, sister, it all comes down to this: when you *know* you got it goin' on, there *is* no need to compete. And since everyone is unique, it's always going to be an apples-to-oranges comparison between any two individuals—in other words, there *is* no comparison because there is only one of you in the world. Just think, if you were already with the Man of Your Dreams, wouldn't you smile and mentally applaud those other happy couples? Of course you would. Cultivating some of that euphoria right now is your ticket to the MANifestival. You can begin by deciding that you're *worthy* and desirous of feeling that good.

Feeling unworthy or self-judgmental is one of the most prevalent forms of Resistance. I'm sure you've already heard from a variety of sources that self-esteem is integral to a healthy, happy life, and how self-love is the bomb-diggity. But what you might not realize is that, while self-esteem is essential for keeping you *out of* unsatisfying or even abusive relationships, unhealthy levels of Resistance prevent you from entering *into* a satisfying one.

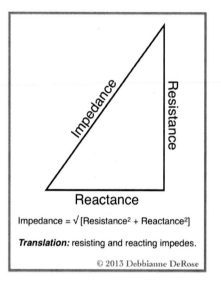

Ceasing and Desisting with the Resisting

"The process of alignment has to do with correlating, harmonizing or aligning what we want with what we actually pay attention to."
—Rick Jarrow

In electrical jargon, *impedance* is what slows down the current, and impedance has two main components: *resistance* and *reactance*. In terms of our mental circuitry, the less Resistance we generate, the more *conducive* we are to the full throttle of energy that life has to offer us— including guidance from our Higher Mind, and pleasing manifestations.

Impedance = √ [Resistance² + Reactance²]

Translation: resisting and reacting impedes.

© 2013 Debbianne DeRose

Most of us humans are masterful Resistors, largely unaware of our considerable talents. But once we've seen the light, we can amp up our vibrations and successfully MANeuver into more preferred realities.

We are Resisting when we overstep our role in the MANifestation process by attempting to wrangle the "how, where, who, and when" details away from Higher Mind. We're also Resisting when we give extra attention to anything we don't like. I say "extra" because a certain amount of attention is necessary to identify the preference, but dwelling on our dislikes beyond the noticing stage is Resistant behavior.

Whether we say it out loud or just think it, a *need* for things to be different—from however we're currently perceiving them to be—is at the heart of Resistance. It's pushing against "what-is," or whatever is currently flowing through our experience.

We may not *like* or *prefer* what we're noticing, but focusing on it only makes it grow. That's because there is no such thing as a Law of Repulsion. Giving energy to what you don't prefer creates interference or static that conflicts with and cancels out your other signals—your orders for stuff you *do* prefer.

When you decide to make peace with the "what-is-ness" of the moment, you invite change into your world. It doesn't mean you're endorsing "what-is"; you just stop *reacting* to it. Being okay with your present single-woman reality doesn't mean you're signing up to remain single the rest of your days. Hell, you've already felt that way at times, right? So, what have you got to lose in implementing my advice?

When you feel empowered and confident in your ability to *allow* a pleasing MANifestation into your life, you *know* that being single is just a temporary condition, so there's no need to rail against it. If you don't quite *know* that yet, then decide to play along—say, for a month—and *act as if* it's true. That's enough time to cultivate new habits, reap the benefits, and initiate a major shift.

When you play the game in this new, more dignified way, your dislikes slowly move down in ranking on the Cosmic Kitchen's prep sheet. So, you'll experience less and less of those unpreferred realities (yay!). In time, stuff you dislike will fade away to a pinpoint and drop out of sight. You'll forget all about it until one day, something triggers the memory out of the blue. But by then, it'll no longer bug you. You'll laugh and appreciate the progress you've made.

I bet you've heard this seemingly ironic Law of Attraction principle: "You can have what you want, as long as you don't really want it." WTF!? Is the Universe some sort of sadist?

Of course you *want* to meet the Man of Your Dreams and enter into a satisfying relationship. The point is not to deny that you want what you want. But when you *need* your desires to materialize and refuse to be happy until they do, well, honey, you're looking through the wrong end of the telescope. You are *impeding* your MANifestation in a big bad way. Two ways, actually: Resisting and Reacting.

You're not alone, if that's your deal—this is typical. It's the form of Resistance known as, *"Weh! Where's my stuff?!,"* and it's usually accompanied by strong Reactance (a grown-up equivalent of stomping your feet or holding your breath).

By frequently taking stock of your "what-is-ness" and generating a status report that says, "Yup, I'm still here at Point A, but Point B is where I *ought* to be... ," you are giving airplay to both Point A and Point B. If you repeatedly think and talk about the fact that you're still single but wanting to be hooked up, what do you suppose the Cosmic Waitress is writing down and serving you? *Single and wanting.*

Perhaps you've been assuming that the Universe would straighten things out on your behalf—as in "oh, come on, you know what I mean." But it doesn't work that way. You have to clean up your own act and provide the Waitress with crystal clear, unambiguous instructions. That means omitting Resistant items from your order, so the Cosmic Chef can whip up some Man-cuisine that really makes your mouth water. It's what you want, and it's what I want for you as well, so *please* quit mucking up the kitchen equipment with all that emotional Reactance.

When you experience negative feelings, emotional guidance is letting you know that the thoughts you were just thinking are out of whack with your integrity. This is golden information, because you have the power to change your thoughts. Contrary to popular indulgence, negative emotion is not a bummer—it's a helping hand. It's like a dashboard light indicating that your car needs fixing. Would you rather disconnect the light and drive recklessly? Do you believe that ignorance is bliss—or that knowledge is power?

If you feel frustrated because your desires have not yet materialized, this indicates the presence of doubt. You doubt that the goods are en route. But *doubt is not a lack of trust*, as it's often defined. Doubt is actually trust in something you don't prefer, and that's why it feels bad. We are always trusting or believing in *something*, or else we wouldn't be having a physical reality experience at all. So it's not that you need to cultivate trust, as you might have previously assumed. You just need to figure out what it is you are unconsciously placing your faith in. Then, as you release the beliefs and definitions that no longer serve you, you become free to *consciously* define your experiences and *consciously* choose what you prefer to believe in.

FUNDAMENTAL TRUTH #5

DOUBT IS NOT A LACK OF FAITH. IT IS TRUSTING IN SOMETHING YOU DON'T PREFER.

But don't be hard on yourself about any of this. If you can approach the subject of where-things-currently-stand with regard to where-you-prefer-to-be in such a way that feels good, you are a rare human being indeed. Most of us are quick to dip into NegativeLand when we compare our unpreferred Present to our preferred Future. When you step into your mastery, it will be easy to appreciate the waiting game, but until then, it's best to avoid generating the status report altogether, or at least quickly turn the page when the report is laid across that desk in your mind's eye.

Keep in mind, too, when you grow impatient, that the built-in time delay for thoughts to manifest is what makes the Earth game so challenging, and presumably that's why you wanted to play. *You can do this.* Women are bad-asses — we birth babies and stuff, remember?

Speaking of time, the Cosmic Café is a little bit like Las Vegas: devoid of clocks, windows or any other indication of time. There is only the Now. Which is why metaphysical teachers always urge us to frame our requests in the present tense such as, "I am in a mutually loving relationship with a beautiful man," rather than future contingencies like, "I would be happy if…" or "I will be so happy when…"

The most powerful orders you can place, therefore, are pure images of you *already* in your desired state, accompanied by some strong good-feeling emotion. Whenever you find yourself in the right frame of mind for such high-quality ordering, milk it for all it's worth. Make the most of your high-vibe situation. Otherwise, when there's too much static on your MANifestation-Station, get into the habit of changing the channel.

Next, let's have a closer look at that static and what's generating it. Resistance comes in many flavors, but *sour grapes* is by far the most popular…

73

Are you swimming in the 7 Cs?

"If you really want to be responsible for your life,
then you've got to be responsible for your mouth."
—*Louise L. Hay*

If you've been lolling about in any of these Cs on a regular basis, you've definitely got some Resistance. The good news is, the sooner you see how you're bucking the current, the sooner you can change course and come ashore.

Complaint

"I hate it when men are too cheap to pay the bill."
"These flaccid guys never even ask for a girl's number."

Remember, there is no Law of Repulsion—every thought attracts. You may be repulsed by something, but if you keep squawking about it, the Cosmic Waitress interprets that as a request for more of the same. Consider this clever and truthful observation from T. Harv Eker: *"When you're complaining, you become a living, breathing crap magnet."*

Cliché

"Always a bridesmaid, never a bride (sigh)."
"All the good ones are taken... or gay."

We often say things like this robotically in our society. So what's the harm in it, besides being boring? Well, if you say it often enough, you might just convince yourself that it's true. Your mind is a powerful tool, and you wouldn't use power tools while you're "asleep," would you?

Criticism

"I'm too overweight. Why would a man want me?"
"Oh my god, I can't believe he said that. What a dork."

What sort of man might you attract if you engage in a lot of criticizing? Do you want a man who agrees with you? Is the Man of Your Dreams a sparring partner? Or a spineless wonder? Neither, I'm guessing. Why not become more of the Love you want to attract?

Contrariness

"Her new man looks good on paper, but we'll see..."
"Our date was fun, but he'll probably never call again."

Is your naysaying justified by so-called "realism"? Could it be your ego's way of protecting you? Consider trading in the "yes, but..." for a pure "yes" more often.

Copping Out

"Well, I don't really need a man anyway."
"I'd rather be single than end up like her."

How is this different from a little kid who, upon learning that he didn't make the cut for a club or team, remarks smugly, "I didn't really want it anyway"? It's an ego-riffic defense, and a sign that Physical Mind is taking over. If you see a woman in a cringeful relationship and conclude that you'd rather stay single, have you considered that there *might* just be other options besides the two your Physical Mind perceives? Maybe it's time for some new role models. At any rate, it pays to remove your focus from the things you *don't* prefer in your reality, and place it on the things you *do*.

Competition

"How did *she* get that guy? She's not even that pretty."
"I might have wrinkles but at least I don't look like *that*."

The need to cut down other women indicates personal insecurity, or a belief in Man-scarcity—or a bad habit. The good news: all of the above are non-fatal and changeable.

Calculation

"I don't really want to go, but it's a good way to meet men."
"There won't be any single guys my age at the party."

Have you ever seen those corny novelty signs that plumbers and other contractors sometimes have, listing their hourly rate plus another, higher rate if the customer helps? Yeah, it's like that. Meddle if you must, but it'll cost you some.

And let's not forget **Commiseration**. When your friends, family, co-workers or other peeps are swimming in the 7Cs, do you jump in with them, contributing your own sob stories or victim-venom to the mix because it's easier than changing? Are you behaving like a pack-animal at your own expense? I know, there's a lot of societal pressure to conform to the negative norm. But consider these wise words from Marianne Williamson:

> *"Your playing small does not serve the world.*
> *There is nothing enlightening about shrinking so*
> *that other people won't feel unsure around you."*

And if you're the class clown type, self-deprecating humor can be hilarious, but there may come a time when you need to level with yourself. Are the jokes really harmless, or are they eroding your self-esteem and generating Resistance within you?

In short, *are you using your powers for good or evil?* I'm just playing with you here, because I don't actually subscribe to that whole "good vs. evil" concept. But it's important to note that this 7Cs stuff has everything to do with personal contentment, and nothing whatsoever to do with intimations of morality or judgment. So, please don't give yourself any crap for participating in the Cs. That would just be piling on more criticism, right? We are all human here. But we're consciously choosing to change. If anything, pat yourself on the back for taking initiative toward a better you.

This process is all about following emotional guidance to better-feeling places. It's *not* about being motivated by any slippery cultural ideals of what it means to be a "good person." Your personalized internal guidance is far more effective than other people's opinions in getting you where you want to go. So, basically, it just plain *feels* better when you let go of those old negative thought patterns. In time, it becomes clear that they don't really hold water anyway.

Happiness is its own reward. It also breathes space into your life for the materialization of your desires, as you become more of a true vibrational match to the goods. You might conclude, after reading this book, that it's nothing but an elaborate ruse to get you to be happy. And you wouldn't be wrong. *Happy* is the place where all the good stuff comes a-knockin'—and finds you, chillin' with your feet up and a cocktail in your hand. *"One's ships come in over a calm sea,"* said Florence S. Shinn, and that includes your Dreamboat.

So, are you tired of floundering in the 7Cs—gasping for air? Ready to come ashore? Here, I'll throw you a rope…

Tow Lines and Flotation Devices

*"Practice develops interactive skills that free us
from acquired conditioned responses."*
—Stan Wrobel

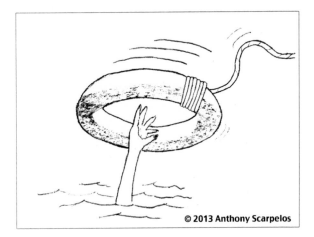

© 2013 Anthony Scarpelos

Good ol' fashioned Willpower

You'll need this no matter what, but for most people, intention alone will not be sufficient to re-route the mental circuits. Maybe you're scoffing at this right now, thinking: "yeah, right, if it were just a matter of willpower, I'd be where I want to be already." Well, maybe, but then again, maybe not. If you're learning new ideas and changing, you've got some new fodder for applying your Will. No need to recycle the Past into the Future. You're like Rocky, growing stronger.

Think of all the superheroes out there who do amazing things because they've set their minds to it—athletes, self-made entrepreneurs, brave souls, obsessive lunatics—and use the inspiration to jump-start your own willpower-motor.

Rehearse your Comeback

When comedians get heckled on stage, they usually have a clever comeback—something to blurt out and prevent the show from becoming a disaster. If you think of the negative voices in your head as your own personal hecklers, how are you going to handle them next time? Since you know their shtick, you can anticipate and outsmart them. For example...

"Uhh, thanks, but no thanks."

"That was then. This is now."

"Stop! Cancel! Clear! Delete!"

"Thanks for your help. You can run along now."

"I'm changing... and changing the channel."

"I don't think that way anymore."

"That was the old me. I'm different now."

"Thank you for sharing. Duly noted... and ignored."

"Everything is possible, and everything changes."

Pivot like a Boss

Emotional pivoting is an art worth cultivating. It involves catching yourself in the negativity act and choosing different thoughts that feel better—thoughts that work *for* you, rather than against you.

*"Turn your attention to what you **do** want... the negative attraction will stop; and in the moment the negative attraction stops, the positive attraction will begin."*
—Abraham-Hicks

Consider this simple but provocative statement from Milton Katselas: *"Praise is the antidote for blame."* If you observe blameful thoughts swirling around in your head, you can transform them into praise by finding something to appreciate about the very same person or situation. The about-face in your energetic state is likely to surprise you. For every negative thought, there is an antidote—a way to turn things around—make it your mission to find it.

79

Here is a basic pivoting recipe:

1. **Intend to pivot.** In general, that is, *before* you find yourself in some trying situation. Imagine you're quickly switching from old knee-jerk reactions to new thoughts about the same topic, and shifting to a better-feeling state of mind in the process. Use an affirmation, if you like: "I can pivot on a dime, any time." In other words, make a *commitment* to yourself that you will opt for change and that you'll keep the ego in check as best you can. You may want to post little reminders or carry a card with you that prompts you to pivot during real-life scenarios that arise.

2. **Be aware of your thoughts and feelings.** Recognize opportunities for pivoting. Any time you experience feelings that are less than blissful, you're on pivoting training ground. Commit to becoming increasingly aware.

3. **Start pivoting.** This should be a no-brainer, but it is truly amazing how many people will read about stuff and never actually apply it. Do the work, reap the rewards. Simple!

4. **Keep doing it.** Like anything else in Life—learning to play an instrument, drive a car, or read and write—there may be an awkward interval before it becomes second nature. Yes, a certain amount of discipline is required initially, but isn't the Man of Your Dreams worth a little effort?

5. **Apply it to more and more things.** It actually gets easier because the better you begin to feel, the more you want to continue feeling that way. It's a benign addiction.

If at first you're pivoting in fits and starts, that's perfectly okay. Any pivoting is better than no pivoting. Levity helps tremendously, if you have access to it. Reach for whatever you can gracefully pull off, because overreaching tends to backfire. Your objective is one baby step at a time in a new direction, not quantum jumping to all-out bliss. But if you want a default goal, aim for the A-list.

Pro-active re-Programming

Thinking negatively may be an old habit, but we have the power to change. When we choose new positive thoughts, we're forging new "thought pathways," and retraining neural networks in our brains to fire differently. It's a lot like a record that skips (pardon my antiquity), stuck in a groove—you have to pick up and reposition the needle.

the Vibrational A-list
Acceptance
Appreciation
Amusement

In addition to changing thoughts case-by-case and on-the-fly via pivoting, you can turbocharge your efforts by doing some deliberate self-brainwashing. I'm talking affirmations, self-hypnosis, auto-suggestion. Does that stuff give you the creeps? Or do you think affirmations are passé or ineffective?

Actually, we are all constantly affirming things in our heads and hypnotizing ourselves all day long. Have a listen inside your head—it's crazy in there, I tell you. So why not take deliberate control over the content and broadcast a new self-program that better suits the new you?

Affirmations, when customized for you, recorded in your own voice, and listened to regularly, *will* effect some startling changes. The key to success lies in crafting your statements so they're *relevant for you and your particular issues*, keeping things in the present tense and focused on positive concepts and wordings only. The mind takes things literally, just as the Cosmic Waitress does (hmmm... do you detect a double-identity?). Since there's a treasure trove of

81

resources out there about working with affirmations, I have just two more words to say: *use them*. I use AffirmMantras as a hybrid tool—an affirmation wielded like a mantra to drown out unwanted mind-blather.

Advance energetic Planning

It's a fine idea to anticipate situations that are likely to challenge your resolve. Like social events choked with couples, holidays, seeing or hearing about your ex, hanging with Notoriously Negative Nellies or interacting with people who tend to ask prying questions about your personal life. If you plan ahead, you can take a minute to define your ideal scene and visualize things going well. Imagine yourself feeling happy and smiling, and easily fielding prickly subjects. Just don't get attached to your preferred scenarios —set it up in your mind, but then fahgeddaboudit.

This planning thing is more potent than you might think. We usually go on auto-pilot and let the chips fall where they may, but once you make a habit of "segment-intending" like this, life becomes remarkably different. It helps you to re-discover just how powerful you are.

Have a look under the Hood

Do you feel like you're on board with all this positive intention stuff, but for some inexplicable reason, things keep going awry? When conscious choice is repeatedly derailed, it's likely there's an unconscious program overriding surface logic. In that case, it's time to inspect your beliefs. Belief systems are the metaphoric bedrock from which we operate, but don't worry—they're far from being set in stone.

Coming Clean

"As water will freeze into the form that it is poured, so mind will solidify only into the forms that our thought takes."
—*Ernest S. Holmes (1919)*

We all have beliefs through which we "filter" our reality. If you feel caught in a Groundhog Day cycle, it might be time to clean the screen. Don't be afraid to open up the control panel of your mind—it doesn't have to be daunting, or left to the "experts."

Sometimes people get so zealous about positive thinking (at least on the surface) that they develop severe allergies to anything that remotely smacks of negativity. But more often than not, they're just sweeping unsavory things under the rug. Strong emotional Reactance indicates the presence of unconscious beliefs, and those beliefs can be identified and released. The more willing you are to face your demons, so to speak, the sooner you can bid them adieu. Consciously identifying beliefs and definitions allows you to bring them into the light and onto the examination table.

Beliefs are essentially crystallized thoughts embedded in the mind that become our basic operating system software. They account for so much of what we experience in life, wanted or unwanted, and yet they remain largely invisible to us. Like so many stubborn clumps of granular detergent, they can *seem* insoluble—unless, of course, you decide to break 'em down.

Beliefs are formed over time by repetitive thoughts we think in response to our observations, like so many layers of dead dinosaurs turning to shale. But you can drill down and harness all that latent energy to fuel your happiness.

Beliefs that don't serve your higher good—which are the lion's share of them—make themselves known by the uncomfortable emotions they engender. These "false truths" are acquired through misunderstandings—often during childhood, though not exclusively so.

Are you rolling your eyes, thinking this sounds like so much pop psychology blah-blah-blah? Well, there's a reason for its popularity. And just to be clear, I'm not advocating the old blame-your-parents gag, nor the wallow-in-it-for-24-months-of-talk-therapy routine. Nope, I'm just lobbying for some efficient personal sleuthing in the spirit of MANifesting. A happier, more effective medium between the self-indulgent pity party and consummate denial.

Okay, here's the deal. We humans tend to operate rather unconsciously, and our beliefs have an insidious way of reinforcing themselves by generating new "evidential" experience to match them. We typically mistake this internalized personal process for "what is"—as if it is some objective "outside" reality that we, as astute citizens, are merely observing, responding to, and commenting on. But we are the ones actually generating the experience in the first place! This cycle explains why so much contentious debating goes on in the world: many people assume that their personal version of reality is universal to all, or that it *should* be. In actuality, personal reality is custom-made for and by each one of us.

Let's say for example that, somewhere along the line you acquired a belief that "men cannot be monogamous." Possibly from hearing your grandmother say it a bunch of times, or seeing your parents fight over it, or perhaps on account of your first lover cheating on you, or maybe you've got some epic run-ins with philanderers in other lifetimes? It doesn't really matter how the belief was forged.

So, in this hypothetical case study, you go about your busy life, and you observe, among many other things, a variety of life situations involving men. Running behind the scenes, your belief acts as a filter for the information you *perceive*. So you end up *seeing* a lot of wandering eyes and *hearing* evidence of an inordinate amount of male transgression—more so than other people who witness the same scenes but do not share your belief. Of course, they have *their own beliefs* to contend with, so they're viewing the same events through other filters with different themes.

THE HUMAN SPIN CYCLE.

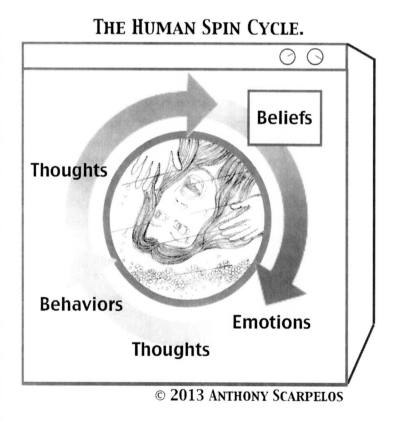

© 2013 ANTHONY SCARPELOS

You experience uncomfortable feelings because your belief that "men cannot be monogamous" is being activated. Feeling shitty is your clue that the belief is not working for you. In other words, it's an *untruth* for you.

So you keep noticing more of these shifty Casanovas and feel increasingly bothered by what you are perceiving. You express discontent whenever the topic arises—and it just so *happens* that it's a topic on the rise in your life.

Now you've added emotional lighter-fuel. More flagrant and frequent flare-ups of male debauchery show up at every turn of your personal reality. Next, you catch your new boyfriend looking at that cute young thang in a certain way, and you're enraged. Then the phone rings and it's your ex (who cheated on you) or it's your best friend, sobbing that her husband has been having an affair.

It's very easy and natural, then, to arrive at the simplistic conclusion that "men cheat." And it's really no surprise because that was the original program running the circuitry.

Of course it is true that *some* men cheat—not all, but some. How many? That is a "what-is" statistic that's completely irrelevant. It doesn't matter because you only want one. And if "cheater" is not on your Man-list, then you have no business focusing your attention on men who *do* cheat. Your unexamined belief was keeping your attention stuck on a subject that is not part of your true self, and the negative feelings were the dashboard light letting you know that something "under the hood" needs your attention.

You can get unstuck and emerge from the spin cycle, and it's easier than you might think. Beliefs tend to dissipate readily in the light of day, once identified; merely seeing and airing them out usually does the trick. Unless, of course, you believe that it's not possible. If a situation seems to call for a "deeper cleaning," that just means there are additional beliefs, still clinging to the mind, that need to be identified. But there's no need to define the work as grueling, or yourself as "broken." Those are just more beliefs, see? Why not define false-belief shedding as exciting and satisfying?

An interesting tenet of Life is that we are always moving *toward pleasure* and *away from pain*. This is true despite the fact that often we appear to do the exact opposite. Our behavior can seem nonsensical and self-sabotaging to us on the *conscious* level—like getting with inappropriate men over and over again. Or staying single when you want to be hooked up. Staying broke when you want to be rich, or miserable when you want to be blissed-out. The paradox lies in our *definitions* of pleasure and pain. If you keep choosing a known crappy situation over a new option, it's because you're defining the unknown as being more painful. We may have borrowed beliefs and definitions from other people such as our parents, but we are the ones building those belief systems within our own psyches.

Beliefs often seem illogical and ridiculously simple. When exposed for the frauds they are, we may find it hard to *believe* that something so dumb and clearly untrue could possibly be the source of our troubles. But it really is that simple! And that voice that insists, "no, it can't be that simple" is the ego-intellect—the same character who spurs you to self-sabotage in the name of protection—so don't let it put up a roadblock in your journey.

FUNDAMENTAL TRUTH #6

LIFE COMES TO US AS A BLANK SLATE AND WE ASSIGN MEANING AS WE GO, COLLECTING BELIEFS LIKE GIRL SCOUT BADGES.

Here's another case study, this one from my personal files. For years, I kept attracting men who didn't want to be in a long term relationship. Some were non-committal—you know, just sort of keeping their options open. Others were too young, geographically inconvenient, or unsuitable for me in some other way. Some were overtly rebellious of anything that hinted of commitment—like making plans for next week. Then there were countless would-be suitors who never even called.

As long as I remained submerged in this cycle, I couldn't see the forest for the trees. I took each situation at face value without perceiving the overall pattern. I responded with Resistant thought energy and Reactance to what I didn't like (unavailable men) and—surprise!—got more of the same in return.

That is, until I finally saw clearly what I was doing. It turns out I had a belief that said "if I get into a long term relationship, I will lose myself and give up my independence." Aha! Doesn't it make sense that with a directive like that in effect, I would chose situations that don't run the risk of losing myself? I mean, who's chomping at the bit to lose her independence? Certainly not me.

But the risk was literally all in my head. There was no need for me to lose myself by entering a committed relationship. Losing the *untruth* was the solution. Once I identified the belief and saw through it, I was able to have my cake and eat it too. Everything becomes possible when you drop beliefs that confine you and define certain things as impossible.

It really is quite simple, and the crucial work we're doing here is coming clean with ourselves. You might be motivated by your Dreamboat but I assure you, once you succeed in liberating some significant false beliefs—particularly core beliefs—it's going to spill over into every aspect of your life in some big, beautiful and unexpected ways.

So, two main approaches to identifying beliefs are:

1. *Notice emotional reactions when they bubble up.*
2. *Take stock of overall patterns or themes in your life.*

Timing is important. Either method requires you to be in a certain calm, objective state of mind. If you're currently experiencing an emotional reaction to something, it's best to make a note of it and attempt the belief work later when that smoking gun has cooled. But the emotional guidance itself is bulletproof: *negative reactions point to false beliefs.*

Of course, it's also true that hormonal, chemical, biological, and physiological factors can cause you to feel less than spectacular and give you that general malaise. And since all our experiences have thought-energy blueprints, you may want to inspect your beliefs and definitions regarding *that* subject matter too. But the sort of negative feelings we're talking about here are the ones that come quickly on the heels of a thought. The process may be so knee-jerk and rapid-fire that you have to break it down, like time-lapse photography, into frames.

Be patient, but persistent, and you'll strike gold. Be open to answers that show up in all sorts of ways—perhaps in a dream, or an overheard conversation in which a stranger speaks your solution. Naturally, your Higher Mind is eager to help you shed your baggage and will be as creative as possible in getting you the information. You only need to remove any blinders or ear plugs you've been sporting.

Out, damned spot!

"Relax, all right? My old man is a television repairman.
He's got this ultimate set of tools. I can fix it."
—Jeff Spicoli in "Fast Times at Ridgemont High"

Ready to dive in? If you're feeling pretty good and can be reasonably objective, take this deductive procedure for a spin.

Finding & Eliminating Beliefs

1. Identify the self-sabotaging behavioral pattern or negative emotional Reactance.

2. Acknowledge that you are choosing to feel or behave this way, and that it actually does serve you, though it may not be obvious at first or logical.

3. Ask yourself, "what would I need to believe is true, in order for this to serve me?"

4. Brainstorm all possible beliefs. If the "aha!" doesn't show up right away, be patient. Meditate on the issue, watch for signs, and enlist the help of a wise friend if possible.

5. Try on beliefs until you find one that fits.

6. Look your old belief in the eye, have an honest talk, thank it for serving you, but let it know that its services are no longer needed.

7. Decide what you now prefer to believe. Reinforce it with Affirmations if you like. Take it for a spin with practice scenarios.

Let's run through an example.

1. "I always fall for the "love 'em and leave 'em" type of guy, and the love affairs never last very long."

2. Say and write: "I *choose* to attract and date men who love 'em and leave 'em because it *serves* me."

3. What would I need to believe is true, in order to *benefit* from being involved with love 'em and leave 'em types?

4. Brainstorm: "I will lose my freedom if I get into a relationship. He will leave me. I will get involved with someone I do not truly love and feel trapped. If he stays with me, there must be something wrong with him. If he gets too close, he'll see the real me..."

5. Aha! Found it. It's this one: "he will leave me... and I'll be worse off than I am now."

6. "I see how I was just trying to protect myself from suffering (and how the Law of Attraction brought me more "love 'em and leave 'em" experiences according to my crystalized thoughts) but I don't need to do this anymore. I now choose to believe that I can be happy, indefinitely and no matter what. It's okay to feel vulnerable in Love."

7. Possible Affirmations: "It's safe to give and receive love. I create my own happiness. I trust myself. There is no end to Love. I'm open to possibilities. I am worthy of Love."

Note that once you've identified the culprit in Step 6, you don't necessarily need to ruminate on its origins in order to clear it out. By realizing that the belief has been with you but that it's *untrue* for you, you simply let it go—like setting a butterfly free from your clasped hands—and in doing so, you set yourself free from its limitations.

Next, you can do some deliberate re-affirming of your new belief, stating to yourself your new policy on the issue. Run through some typical scenarios in your imagination—things you've experienced in the past that often triggered the old behavior and negative emotions. How are things different? How do you act, feel, behave, talk? This is very much like re-writing your personal history—as if you become a new person with a different Past after eliminating those false beliefs. It's truly life-changing if you're really getting to the heart of your belief system. Don't cling to Past identities, whatever they may be—that's just the ego trying to protect you again. You can tell a new story about yourself now, as long as you're not attached to the old one. Don't allow other people to pin you to your old identity either.

In the preceding example, you might imagine meeting another "love 'em and leave 'em" guy, seeing his game clearly, early on, and saying "no thanks!" then feeling very self-satisfied because you now know you're on your way to having a committed, lasting relationship in your life—and perhaps for the first time, you feel that it's really possible.

Choosing to feel appreciative, or even amused, about the whole thing is a fabulous idea. I highly recommend doing the "rinse and repeat" cycle: reapply the same steps to root out *related beliefs* that are still in effect. After all, that's why they call it a "belief system"—it's a collection of interconnected beliefs flowing together like tributaries to a river. They may have been dumping out into the 7Cs until now, but if you commit to change and to self-honesty, you can re-map them toward your ocean of bliss.

Other Methods of Note

I've had superb results using the Lefkoe method (and no, I'm not affiliated with them). It's very effective for eliminating unwanted core beliefs acquired in youth. The term "core beliefs" refers to beliefs that have to do with our basic self-concepts. They create a ripple effect that either enhances or detracts from our quality of Life in every facet. Just think what a completely different life experience a person can have if she believes "I am loved" at the core, versus "I am not lovable." If you're flinching or rolling your eyes right now, the chances are very good that this sort of core belief sleuthing is *exactly* what you need to do. Reactance indicates that your buttons are being pushed, and that your ego is trying to protect you by keeping contentious subjects at bay. So please *do* persevere.

It doesn't take a childhood of egregious abuse to create self-esteem-eroding beliefs. As a little kid, failing to obtain your parents' undivided attention is grounds for concluding "I'm not important." Let's face it, even SuperMom or SuperDad can't give 100% attention to Little You, and most of us were not raised by superheroes. It's a set-up for misunderstandings, this life-as-a-human gag. So if you think this stuff doesn't apply to you, think again. Nearly everyone takes on erroneous core beliefs, and freeing yourself up from them is going to catalyze huge positive changes in you.

The Lefkoes have a website (RecreateYourLife.com) where you'll find some sample process videos. Their method involves, among other things, coming up with alternative explanations for events you observed and drew false conclusions about, and this helps you to expand your point of view and release those erroneous assumptions. For example, you really *are* important, but your parents were just busy when you wanted their attention. Or, heck, maybe your parents didn't actually love you (unlikely, though possible), but that doesn't mean you're not lovable. Your tender young mind was incapable of reasoning and keeping it all in perspective, and that's why we need to make these corrections to our core understandings now. After all, the beliefs we acquired in our early years don't dissipate on their own. Most people are dragging around unnecessary burdens their whole lives. Don't you want out of that club?

Of course, belief-generating is not confined to childhood. Any time we observe the world and draw half-truthful conclusions—defining our perceptions in some limited way—we add to our collection of beliefs. With so many perspectives available, why not begin to consciously choose empowering beliefs—ones that feel good?

Another terrific tool is EFT, the Emotional Freedom Technique, a unique East-meets-West multi-purpose healing modality. You tap with your fingers on acupuncture points on your body while verbally communicating with your unconscious mind. I've used it many times, both on my own and with the help of a talented practitioner, and had amazing success in several different applications—including shifting my beliefs about men and relationships (you can read more about that in *What I Did On My Midlife Crisis Vacation*). There's a growing bounty of how-to information and EFT success stories out there for your perusal.

Unlike the other methods I've described, the tapping actually works well when you're in the throes of strong emotion—that is, while the belief is being activated. It drains the emotional charge off a hot topic within seconds. EFT is harmless, has no side effects or risks... well, other than looking silly if someone happens to catch you in the act, but I'm pretty sure it's worth it.

94

I am that: the yin and the yang of things

"Thought is a magnet, and the longed-for pleasure,
or boon, or aim, or object, is the steel."
—Frances L. Warner

I once heard Wayne Dyer say that we attract into our lives not what we *desire*, but what we *are*. And maybe that's true, in some general sense. I had to become more accepting and loving, and less judgmental, in order to attract such a loving, accepting, and non-judgmental man as Tony into my life. And looking back ten, twenty, or even just a few years ago, I definitely was not qualified. I suppose I had to become closer to my ideal self, or the Woman of My Dreams, in order to attract the Man of My Dreams.

In another sense, we mate with our opposites—in lots of little ways, and certainly in terms of gender (well, if you're doing the hetero thing, that is). But regardless of gender, each of us has feminine and masculine energies, or yin and yang, within us. The particular custom blend in which these energies are expressed is unique to each individual. It's a dynamic thing, a sort of dance, a continual shifting of poles, and a microcosm of the Dualism present in all of Life. The people we attract are essentially a match to our particular yin/yang recipe at the time—not necessarily a carbon copy, but more like a mirror image.

Years ago, my single girlfriends and I often complained about how wimpy all the dudes were. We bitched about them never asking us out, never making a move, and generally not having enough testosterone for our tastes. We saw it as a matter of *fact* and impartial observation, and wondered out loud if our geographic area had been stricken with a high incidence of this particular man-crime.

Meanwhile, several energy healers I patronized detected a sort of energetic misappropriation in me. Heck, I detected it myself at times—a left/right imbalance, and what might be considered an abundance of yang with regard to yin. But it's amazing how brilliant information can sometimes fall upon deaf ears. I guess I just had to ride it out and figure it out in my own stubbornly independent fashion.

I'd been remodeling houses, slinging power tools, shlepping lumber, and generally doing everything in a knock-down drag-out yang-ish way every chance I got. Not that masculinity is confined to such stereotypical activities; it was merely an overt display of my inner state. It's pretty comical that I was literally building physical walls and structures with my hands while re-mortaring the emotional ones within. I was taking DIY (do-it-yourself) culture to extremes, and there was little or no space for a Man inside my chateau-built-for-one.

By now, you've probably reached the same "aha" or "duh" that took me years to uncover: *of course* the dudes in my reality-sphere were wimpy. Who else does an over-the-top YangWoman draw in but extreme-wussy YinMen? And it happened repeatedly, due to my ongoing Resistance (observing and commenting on what-is) and Reactance (feeling annoyed). That's just Law of Attraction 101. Which, naturally, is what also plunked me down in the same canoe with vibrationally-matched womenfolk for commiseration purposes as we paddled upstream together.

The way this imbalance eventually got "fixed" was me embracing my feminine side, for lack of a better way to put

96

it (and sorry about the gag-me cliché). In practical terms, that meant learning to relinquish control, trust other people (and the Universe) more and cultivate *receptivity*. In other words, no longer doing things the maximum-effort way, but easing into a more relaxed state where I *allow* things to happen. I had to admit to myself that I didn't *need* to go it alone anymore, that I *shouldn't* go it alone, and that ultimately, none of us *ever* really does anything alone.

Forgive me for waxing anthropological for a moment here, but it seems to me that, over the epochs, an enormous pendulum swings back and forth, and perhaps we're still in the process of recovering from the latest oscillation. Broadly speaking, women had been less than fully empowered for centuries, and since the 1960s and '70s (in the U.S. at least), women's equality has really started cookin'. Could it be that some of us—both women and men—are still adjusting and fine-tuning our yin-yang recipes? Although I was only born in the '60s, presumably I soaked up some "stuff" from prior generations and used it as fodder for my belief systems. But thanks to introspection and energy healing, I've been actively shedding those unnecessaries for the past few years. Whether this theory holds true or not doesn't much matter, but I offer it for thought-food.

What I do know for sure is that *letting men be men*—permitting them to fill their desired and probably hard-wired roles—is a highly underrated practice amongst us modern women. We're so powerful that some of us get into the habit of doing everything for ourselves—just because we can. Or because we *need* to... but remember, we created the reality of that need in the first place. We get accustomed to the solo life and don't always realize that we're putting up invisible walls. The antidote is freeing up space for a Man, both physically and energetically—rolling out the psychic welcome-mat.

If you've been on your own for a while, begin now to use your imagination during regular everyday activities to imagine a Man in your life. For instance, you're sitting at the table eating breakfast, and *he's* sitting there too, maybe reading or drinking coffee—whatever realistic details please you. Some gals use an extra place setting as a physical prop. Do whatever works for you, but do it a few times a day, in varied scenarios. The goal is to cultivate the *feeling* of being together. There's no need to visualize big dramatic romantic scenes; your accumulated small-scale envisionings are plenty powerful. Oh, and don't forget to have fun with it.

MAN POINTER #3

USE YOUR IMAGINATION TO INCORPORATE THAT HOOKED-UP FEELING INTO EVERYDAY LIFE.

The *Mama Gena* books (see the Recommended Reading section) constitute a festive refresher course in the proper use of our god-given chick-assets: reclaiming and reveling in our yin-power while allowing the menfolk to shine. Her playful, sassy take on gender issues is more practical than it might seem at first blush.

I know some women who purposefully wear pink in order to focus on femininity, softness and love. I had made some wardrobe changes myself when I realized I'd been spending most of my time in dirty old baggy work clothes. Treating yourself to some pampering isn't a bad idea, ladies —nor is treating yourself the way you'd like your Man to treat you. I love watching old black-n-white movies with girly girls and manly men of yore. I know, modern life bears little resemblance to cinematic portrayals of the 1940s—and we're mostly glad for that—but it offers a different perspective that can be very helpful (not to mention delightful, when Doris Day is singing.)

If you've been living in that overly yang way as I was, please listen up. Do you tend to strong-arm the dating process (or the would-be dating process that never seems to get off the ground) by taking the lead, being the alpha, pursuing the guy? *Please, for the love of god, STOP DOING THIS!* That is exactly the sort of thing I'm talking about when I say "let the men be men." He *wants* to be the man. And you want him to be the man too. But if you're busy being the man *and* the woman, you put him out of a job, see?

You may get that twitchy feeling if he doesn't call you back after a couple of days, even though he said he would, but you *must* refrain from swallowing up the energetic space between the two of you. Practice the Art of Allowing and the art of *quiet, subtle magnetizing.* Do *not* chase after a man! Instead, draw him unto you. That is the yin way—and oh what a powerful force it is.

Are you afraid you'll run the risk of your Dreamboat sailing away if you don't pick up that phone and *make* things happen? And what if he doesn't call back, not *ever?*

Ground control to female brain: how could he possibly be the Man of Your Dreams if he is so disinterested? Clearly he is not. He is, however, your teacher—helping you learn to relax and trust, and to love yourself more. This shifting is about understanding that your desires *will* be fulfilled, and that you can stop trying so damn hard. It's about finding your balance. And it feels really, really good when you do.

Whew. Okay, that was a lot of tough love. I'm sorry, but it had to be done. How are you holding up? Let's move on to a kinder, gentler subject.

Gratitude Adjustment

"The grateful mind is constantly fixed upon the best;
therefore it tends to become the best;
it takes the form or character of the best,
and will receive the best."
— Wallace D. Wattles

How many times has some New Age spiritual guru harangued you about the importance of adopting an "attitude of gratitude"? You may be relieved to hear that I'm not going to join in that chorus. Well, not exactly. I've got a hair to split.

Appreciation is *not* the same thing as gratitude. Though we often use these terms interchangeably, the vibration and feeling that each word represents is distinctly different. Gratitude usually contains some struggle or inference to an unwanted aspect of the subject. For example, "I'm so grateful that I don't have to deal with *that* anymore." More often than not, gratitude seems to invite comparison and guilt. You start thinking "oh, that guru's got a point... I mean, my life is so good, and other people are suffering, so I *should* be grateful." Well, personally, I'm not a fan of "shoulds" or guilt as motivation. I think it's a dirty trick of the ego, as a matter of fact. As is delving into other people's reality-creations as an excuse to disallow your own desires.

Appreciation, on the other hand, is pure enjoyment. It contains no judgmentalism, no contingency clauses, and no ulterior motive of absolution. It is loving the scent of a flower or the color of a person's eyes, grooving on a song, relishing the taste of some yummy food, basking in the warmth of the sun, nodding at the soundness of a proposed idea. No thing is too small or obscure to appreciate.

According to Abraham-Hicks, Appreciation is defined as, *"the absence of everything that feels bad and the presence of everything that feels good."* It is acceptance mixed with joy. And in its fullest form, everything and everyone in creation becomes perfectly okay, and merely part of this big petri dish we're all in here. If we can don the Goddess-goggles, it's possible to appreciate the very existence and set-up of this clever Earth game we're playing here. But *only* when we're feeling especially bubbly.

Small-scale Appreciation, and its vibration-raising magic, is, however, always available. And while the Physical Mind can get easily carried away, thinking that Appreciation requires us to convert an entire horrific experience into butterflies and smiley faces, it doesn't need to be so grandiose. When you decide to appreciate something, no matter how subtle, you absolutely *do* pivot and shift your vibration significantly. As my friend Kelli says, "Appreciation can turn any situation around, that's for sure."

I suggest playing the Find-Something-To-Appreciate game as often as possible. If you're having a particularly trying day at work, and *that one person* is hassling you again, see if you can sincerely compliment her attire, for example. There's no need to voice it to her unless you really want to. Maybe you like the way she neatly files papers, or her devotion to her kids.

Fed up with the place you're living in? Find *something* you like about it, even if it's just the wall color or the fact that the lights work. Start small and see where it takes you. I guarantee you'll start feeling better.

Feeling upset about something political? Surely you can find things to appreciate. Isn't it great having cholera-free running water in our homes? Even if you go with gratitude initially like that, you're still heading in a helpful direction.

Okay, here's a more advanced Appreciation game. Are you ready? Sometime when you're in the mood, revisit the Ghosts of Relationships Past. Conduct an old-flame inventory, but do the very thing that people are often criticized for doing: *engage in selective memory*. Focus *only* on the parts you like. What can you appreciate about each beau? You may want to modify and enhance your Man-list when the insights come rolling down the pike.

If you can muster a certain amount of objectivity about your romantic experiences, it might just trigger some epiphanies. That's what happened with me. I'd had this one rocky relationship that puzzled me for years; it had seemed like a complete waste of time and energy. Armed with my intent to appreciate something—anything—about him and our time together, all I could muster was "good sex." Well, that turned out to be the gem. I suddenly understood that this otherwise rueful relationship had been the perfect environment for shedding my remaining inhibitions. I saw the gift, and I felt genuine Appreciation. By the way, that's all a miracle really is, according to *A Course in Miracles*: a change in perspective.

Just think how far you've come as a woman, and how your priorities and tastes have evolved over the years. Having all these experiences is how we figure out what we like and don't like. Without darkness, how would we recognize Light? We *need* to have opposing versions of everything, down to the finest detail, to make this dualistic Life game work, and that includes your personal likes and dislikes. Why not *redefine* your life experiences by replacing negative thoughts with Appreciation for the clarity? Anything can be defined as positive with the right attitude.

Since the "what" and "why" of a MANifestation is your domain as a physical being, and since the Physical Mind has a special knack for reviewing and analyzing the Past, this is your time to shine. Review what worked well, what pleased you, what preferences you've developed, and what you'd like to experience but maybe cannot yet imagine. Then hand the files over to your Higher Mind who will further process your case, handling all the details of "who, when, where and how." And ideally, do it all with Appreciation.

Remember how I said that you don't need to believe your Dreamboat even exists? Well, it's still true, and I've got a workaround solution that permits you to forge ahead with the visualizing and appreciating fun. If you can't buy into the idea that one Man embodies all of your desired Man-qualities, focus on one aspect of him at a time. There's a fun diagram and a worksheet you can use.

For example, it may be easy for you to imagine a man who enjoys cooking. So you visualize your Lover-Man chef cooking with or for you, or feeding you—whatever you desire. You watch your favorite Iron Chef hottie on TV. And the next time you visit your sister's house, you admire your brother-in-law happily buzzing around in the kitchen.

At another time, you might focus on appreciating a man who loves spending time with (your) kids. Or who plays baseball. Or who takes walks with you. Whatever's on your list, just take small bites of it. And keep checking in to see how you *feel* because your emotions tell you what's working and what isn't. In the end, your "Franken-Man" will encompass all the parts that truly matter to you.

Have fun patching your Man together! There's a "blank Frank" and blank Appreciating worksheet at the end of the book, and they're downloadable from my website as well.

www.debbianne.com

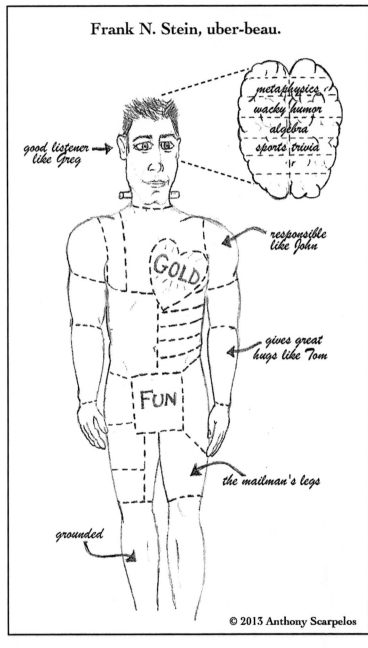

Frank N. Stein, uber-beau.

metaphysics
wacky humor
algebra
sports trivia
r

good listener like Greg

responsible like John

GOLD

gives great hugs like Tom

FUN

the mailman's legs

grounded

© 2013 Anthony Scarpelos

Active Appreciating (example)

Today, I will notice and appreciate pleasing qualities in the world around me, especially in any men I encounter, see, hear, or hear about. I will do my noticing in an organic fashion without scheming, plotting, or fretting. I just intend... and see what happens. This is fun!

Man-list Item 1:   open-mindedness

Scenario 1:   guy on the radio talking about how he started meditating and embracing change

Scenario 2:   my co-worker's brother was really cool when his son came out of the closet

Scenario 3:   my cousin's husband loves to try any kind of food, loves travel and other cultures

Man-list Item 2:   meatsuit! (physicality)

Scenario 1:   admiring the contractor's arms

Scenario 2:   standing behind a guy in line at the store who is the perfect height for me

Scenario 3:   digging this guy on TV, how he carries himself, his posture, eyes and smile

Man-list Item 3:   common interests

Scenario 1:   at the movie theater, noticed some men my age going to watch the same movie as me

Scenario 2:   guy on Facebook likes and comments on the same stuff as me--similar sense of humor

Scenario 3:   my neighbors are out riding their bikes together. They look happy and compatible. yay!

© 2013 Debbianne DeRose

Positivity Posse

"You are the average of the five people you spend the most time with."
—Jim Rohn

You may find yourself thinking that it's difficult to maintain a positive state of mind, and that's understandable, considering the bewildering amount of daily stimuli we're exposed to.

What to do? Well, first of all, stop reinforcing the belief that it's hard. Beyond that, I have to ask you this: what are you programming yourself with? Do you read blogs that bitch and moan about the bleak dating scene (as if there is only *one*) or articles that rattle off statistics about male impotency and other unwanted topics? Are you an avid consumer of doom-and-gloom broadcasts in general?

You may feel the need to stay informed, but there is a huge assortment of information out there. Don't mistake our collective cultural preoccupation with tragedy and victimhood for a fair representation of "what is." There exist infinite possibilities in the "all-that-is," and the popular "all-that-sucks" paradigm just ain't all-a-dat. The happiest people I know tend to distance themselves from mainstream media. I'm not saying you should bury your head in the sand, but you might want to take a closer look at what you're exposing yourself to and what sorts of thoughts it inspires you to think, given that your thoughts are creating your personal reality. You can be *aware* of consensus reality without being overrun by negativity.

What about your peeps? Is your inner circle blessed with an abundance of naysayers and wet blankets? Do you feel "stuck" in relationships with others that are based primarily on gossip and negative chatter?

Sonia Choquette, in *Your Heart's Desire*, likens the conscious manifesting process to gardening. You plant a seed, water it, and wait for it to sprout. But you have to nurture it too, and protect it from various varmints until it's big and strong enough to thrive on its own. If you're feeling vulnerable in the early stages of your deliberate manifesting work, it makes sense to not share your dreams with people who are likely to dump pesticides on them.

I'm not advising you to go around issuing pink slips to your peeps. I am, however, encouraging you to prioritize your own happiness, and that might mean re-allocating with whom and how you spend your time, as least in the early stages. It's your call. You get to choose who gets backstage passes to your psyche. You also get to decide that you're not going to judge yourself for any choices you make.

It would be ideal to surround yourself with friends and family who understand the importance of positive thought, or who at least love, support and respect you even if they don't fully comprehend what you're up to. Deep down inside, most people understand the stuff we've been talking about here, in their own way. They may not speak the metaphysical lingo, but so what? If you approach them with sincerity and love—especially a healthy heaping of *self-love* that commits you to making positive changes—they may surprise you. Just don't ask or require anyone else to change; therein lies the ultimate secret to happiness.

It *is* entirely possible to transform existing difficult relationships into more supportive ones. It's just that in some cases you'd have to be some kind of spiritual bad-ass to pull it off.

So if you're feeling unsupported, why not seek out some new friends to share the journey while you cheer each other on? At the very least, cyber-pals are easy to come by these days, through various Law of Attraction online groups and forums and whatnot. Keep in mind that the real support is entirely within you, but brat packs can serve as nifty permission slips, while providing synergistic fun.

If you do decide to form or join a Law of Attraction (LOA) group, I've got some ideas you might want to try out, in the spirit of good clean giggly girl-fun. It can be a huge help to have some partners in self-improvement crime, because it's too easy to get caught up in a head trip. As long as your peeps are on the same page, let it out, share it, and laugh about it.

One more caveat. It's very easy for well-meaning people to misunderstand each other at times—particularly via texting and emailing when you're not there in the flesh to breathe expression into the electrons. There's a tendency to want to "help" by pointing out each other's "failings" in terms of negative thought. But words can be tricky. The statement, "he's wearing plaid," for example, could be a neutral observation, a joyous occasion, or a blatant case of Resistance—it all depends on who said it, how they meant it in that moment, and what their historical patterns have been. So if in doubt, just offer love, support, humor, and positivity rather than policing services.

Your LOA Brat Pack

♥ Share your lists of Man-qualities, You-qualities, and You-and-Him-qualities with each other. Spend a little time soaking in each item, and share your impressions and visualizations with your friend(s). Having another person lend energy to your MANifesting goals can be quite powerful. Likewise, you'll get a high from giving energy to theirs.

♥ Share your collages and Man-U-Scripts if you're feeling bold. Maybe even act out the script by reading the lines aloud? But only if it's super fun, of course.

♥ Use your imagination to create scenarios and share them with one another. You can do this on the fly if you're in physical proximity to your gal-pals—for example, if you're out having a drink, imagine you're on a double date and your Dreamboats are playing pool in the next room (or out hunting dinner—whatever turns you on). You can also co-create visions with cyber-buddies. When you have friends who are in on the fun, you don't need to worry about being "realistic" or being called out on anything. Play the "Wouldn't-It-Be-Nice-If..." game (see Abraham-Hicks), adding as much detail and good feeling as you can.

♥ Weave your MANifestation, playfully but matter-of-factly, into conversations: "Sandy's getting married next year, and the wedding's going to be so fun because I'll be there dancing with my Man..."

♥ Draw your "Franken-Men" and share them.

Knowing Shit from Shinola

"Say no to the good so that you can say yes to the great."
—Jack Canfield

When you first dive into this woo-woo work, the Cosmic Kitchen may be serving you up more of the "same ol' same old" for a little while. This is pretty typical, and the reason is that, even though your thoughts are changing, there's a certain amount of "echo" from the Past that persists due to the time lag in effect here on Earth. You could consider it a test—if you're the sort of person who takes pride in acing tests. Otherwise, just hang in there. If you are honestly changing your thought patterns, your "outer" experience *must* change, and it will—very soon.

Things are going to start cropping up. Tune into *subtlety*: ways in which familiar old situations now feel different; changes in how others relate to you; the qualities and aspects of people and things your attention is being drawn to; and the experiences you're now becoming privy to. At some point, men will come out of the woodwork—I shit you not. But what *sort* of men? That's what we need to talk about.

Now I know you're excited about the prospects of some hard wood cropping up (heh heh), but initially, the wood that washes upon your shores might be "driftwood"— meaning, a harbinger of your Dreamboat yet to sail in.

Driftwood can fake you out, because it has many of the qualities you're seeking. And yet, something about it is not quite right. There's a deal-breaker in there somewhere. Like, he's married. Or... he has *most* of the redeeming qualities on your Man-list plus one big fat item on your list of annoyances. (If you're thinking you missed something, no, I

110

didn't suggest deliberately making a deal-killer list. It's more productive to focus on the positive flip-side of things, and besides, you know what your personal "no-no"s are, right? Still, some people do swear by it.)

When driftwood emerges, you *must* keep your wits about you. Stay on course—do not be lured onto the rocks! The ability to *discern* is absolutely crucial to receiving what you truly desire. Nevertheless, we know how tricky this can be for women when it comes to Love—maybe because we're genetically or socially conditioned to accommodate others?

Discernment is a major reason for creating a Man-list in the first place—it's a hard copy of your order for reference. Before you elope to Vegas with Mr. Maybe, humor me and do a little role-playing, okay? Pretend you are an overachieving anal-retentive shipping clerk, and verify that the goods actually match the docket.

Seriously, though, when you're legitimately swept off your feet, I'm about the last person who's going to throw cold water on your romance. The main pitfall I'm actually cautioning against is the misappropriation of thought-energy. In short, another form of Resistance.

Chasing after lukewarm prospects, even in the privacy of your own mind, amounts to a squandering of your power. Let me explain by way of example. I have a friend, Megan, who scrutinizes every man-prospect for signs of her unworthiness. If a man she's interested in does not call back right away, she launches into a *"what is wrong with me?"* tirade. In reality, if a guy doesn't call back (barring any highly unusual circumstances to be unraveled later on), he's *not* the Man of Your Dreams. And if a man states that he'll call, there is absolutely nothing for you to do but live your life, be happy, and answer the phone if and when it does ring, then respond accordingly to the caller in the Now.

If days or even weeks go by without a ringy-dingy from this man, wouldn't it be more helpful, more empowering, and a more judicious use of your precious energy to focus on *appreciating* the fact that he's *not* calling and therefore not tying up the line, so to speak, when the Right Mister comes to call? And while you're at it, why not spend some time appreciating yourself?

Megan has two challenges. First, she must establish her self-worth so that it's no longer negotiable. Second, she needs to learn to better recognize The Goods when she sees them, and keep moving otherwise. Literally keeping yourself busy, to the point where you have no time for obsessing, is a fine idea if you're anything like Megan.

Maybe some of us are just hard-wired for monogamy and have that sort of take-no-prisoners, get-it-done project management ethic in us. I don't know, but once we chicks lock a man in the crosshairs, we tend to abandon all reason. I once had a spontaneous flirtation in the supermarket that spurred all sorts of extended mental fabrications—as if liking the same brand of almond milk was grounds for a relationship.

Take my seasoned advice: don't bum-rush the process. Don't scan every prospect to determine whether he's "the One." Aspects of your grand MANifestation show up regularly, in part and parcel, but don't be in a big hurry to piece together your "Franken-Man," because that's not actually your job. It's another case of Physical Mind overstepping her capabilities, attempting to do the job of Higher Mind. P-mind supplies the specifications by focusing on examples of each puzzle piece, and H-mind builds the overall MANifestation out of them. Believe me, when your Man shows up, it will be ridiculously obvious. So in the meantime, stop calling the other guys "Frank," okay?

Your job is to seize opportunities to focus on anything you dig about each dude who shows up in your life. You don't *need* anything from them, like a date or a phone call. It doesn't matter if they're married, old, young, real, fictional, or anything else. You don't *need* any of them to be The One, even if a guy may *appear* to be qualified. You're just using his attributes to revel in some good feelings and fantasize away—in a general, open way, not about him per se.

Does that sound objectionable to be "using" people for your own purposes? It's not, because what you're actually doing is exchanging energy with them. It's a telepathic compliment, bound to elicit smiles and good vibes.

Another misappropriation of your energy involves *readily accepting half-assed attempts to win your affection.* Do I have to go into gory detail? Okay, how about the guy who takes you out but speaks to you in ways that are distinctly insulting or undermining… and you brush it aside or rationalize it. Or the charmer who repeatedly breaks his promises and makes excuses, but you allow him to sweep you up and bowl you over, time and time again. Listen sister, when Love is in the air, there's going to be fireworks and rainbows, not smog and second-hand smoke.

It's as if the Universe is prompting you, "Are you sure about that? Is *this* what you want? Are you *sure?*" When you pass the pop quizzes, you get to move on. When you stand grounded in your clarity, knowing what you want and refusing to settle, these tests will subside, and Mr. Wrong will no longer be a regular on your personal reality show.

Now, you might be thinking: "But I don't want to spoil the romance by being so analytical like that. Anyway, maybe I'm being too nitpicky and I should just get over it already? I mean, nobody's perfect, *right?* I don't want to disqualify a quality man from the running." Well, those are very important questions to ask, and ultimately, *you* are the only one with the answers. Nonetheless, I will attempt a generic clarity-injection.

Yes, of course, no one is "perfect," whatever that means (and if they were, they'd be damn boring... and probably not even human). However, the particular "imperfections" of your SupraLove are more likely to make themselves known later on, and for the express purpose of facilitating your personal growth. And while it is true that various experiments with Mr. Not-Quite-Right do induce growth, it's also true that learning doesn't have to be quite so hard. *Life is supposed to be fun.*

A red flag that pops up early on is just that: *a red flag.* It's that gnawing pain in the belly, when Higher Mind is whispering softly in your ear—or maybe even screaming in it. Race car drivers know what to do when a red flag is waved: *stop the damn car.* We women, on the other hand, tend to smile, wave back and keep on driving. Sure, we see the thing undulating in the wind, but in our mind's eye it's a docile pastel yard flag that reads: "Welcome to your next Man-Project."

Ladies! Are we so starved for sugar that we're sitting in that Cosmic Café trying to alchemize brussels sprouts into chocolate cake? I'll be the first to admit that I did just that—for years. Before meeting Tony, he last guy I was ga-ga over would flake out and not even call me. I wasted time and energy fretting over the situation and wanting things to be different, but in hindsight it was clearly a blessing that he blew me off. He was all kinds of wrong for me, and getting involved with him might have interfered with the real LoveFest that was just around the corner. Higher Mind had it all set up, see? But my Physical Mind engaged in needless angst and silly MANeuverings along the way.

114

I sure would love to help prevent unnecessary detours in *your* Man-trip, if that's possible. The moral I want to impress upon you is this: *alchemy is an esoteric craft reserved for the few.* For the rest of us, it's much easier to re-order and wait for the Cosmic Waitress to bring out the chocolate cake.

When the Right Mister is in your midst, it's going to *feel* right. You won't be second-guessing yourself and rationalizing away red flags. So why not relax and have fun until he arrives?

Mr. Right On might possess certain characteristics that are reminiscent of old What's-his-name, but somehow it will be doable this time: a former pet peeve transformed into a cute endearing quirk. But we're talking relatively minor stuff. Justifying that "things will be different with *this* abusive alcoholic because it just *feels* right" would be a gross misinterpretation of my words, and a prime example of some core beliefs just begging for inspection.

Learn to sort out your rationalizations ("well, I *guess* I like him... I mean, he's got a good job") from the gut's-honest truth as you sift through the Man-offerings. Be open, anticipatory and loving—without becoming over-eager or self-sacrificing.

Another way to frame this discernment idea is to think of yourself as a hip company with a new job opening. You're interviewing candidates—enthusiastically, respectfully—but if someone is grossly underqualified, you simply wish them well. You're not snobbish or arrogant, because you know that every interaction is an equal exchange of value. Anyone who enters our lives does so for a reason, whether or not we consciously understand what that reason is. Some stay longer than others, but in the end it's *all good*.

And while you're following the yellow brick road, consider reading *The Four Man Plan* by Cindy Lu. Even if

115

you don't participate in the plan as she's invented it, it's bound to advance your self-assessed market value while helping you refrain from making snap judgments about Man-prospects.

Yes, that's the pitfall at the other end of the discernment stick: *disqualifying candidates too quickly*. I've heard so many great quirky stories in which happy couples strongly disliked one another at first, but they stuck it out because of a "minimum date rule" or a little voice inside that told them to keep going. Ah, yes, that would be the voice of Higher Mind.

The distinction between those rough-start happily-ever-after situations and genuine red flags is important, and that's where your powers of discernment come into play. When you find yourself hesitating, and it's actually the right Man for you, there is likely to be some flimsy excuse for rejecting him that actually covers up an unconscious process. For instance, maybe you're reluctant to get into a relationship where you might have to deal with your own shit, and you instinctively recognize this person as your mate and try to run away. It's not a red flag, but more like what Cindy Lu calls "being a poopyhead" (refusing a second date because he's wearing pleated pants, for example). *So, is it shit* or *is it Shinola?* Only you know.

MAN POINTER #4

SORT OUT RATIONALIZATIONS FROM THE GUT'S-HONEST TRUTH.

If this whole discernment thing seems challenging because your Spidey Senses have been out of commission for a while, just begin by *intending* to resurrect them. Sweep

116

off the cobwebs and check in with gut-guidance more frequently. Start with things of minor consequence: ask for guidance, be open to answers, and act on your intuition as best you can. Once you get the pump primed, your internal guidance-fount will bubble up more readily. The more you trust, the more guidance you'll *perceive*. And the more guided you are, the happier you'll become. It's a judicious cycle.

One more thing. Please don't think for a nano-second that I'm railing against the idea of you having a snack while you wait for the main course. Some people proclaim that you must "save yourself" (energetically, at least) for your proper mate, and that doing the "friends with benefits" thing dissipates your energy and interferes with the ultimate MANifestation. I'm not so sure that's true across the board. I say only *you* know what the deal is for *you*. Some women can keep a fuck-buddy on the side while maintaining clarity and focus. It just depends on how we feel about the guy, I suppose. Occasionally, friends morph into lovers, and lovers into Dreamboats, but I wouldn't count on it. If y'all have been rolling in the hay for months or years and it hasn't gone there yet, it's seems dang unlikely. Then again, doing your belief inspection and releasing could cause all sorts of monumental changes. This stuff is very personal and unpredictable.

Come to think of it, having some semblance of a sex life is not a bad idea. I mean, it can generate good vibes that work in your favor—*if* your head's screwed on the right way. But that's a big *if*, considering how female hormones can overtake reason faster than the Paparazzi nabs a Scientology scandal. Well, do what you will with your body, but do keep an eye on your mind, so to speak.

Fakin' it 'til we be Makin' it

*"If we want a thing, we must have within ourselves
the mental equivalent before we get it."*
—Ernest S. Holmes

I really *love* dancing. I've been into partner dances like ballroom, swing and salsa for years. When I hear a swingin' jazz tune from yesteryear, I feel almost chemically compelled to get up and bust some Lindy Hop or Charleston moves. But without a partner to lead, I'm dead in the water. Dancing with other chicks, for me, is just… well, awkward and depressing. And though the dance events and classes I attended were usually well-stocked with men, they were just strangers to dance with for a song or two.

I longed for the two-in-one combo: a Lover Man of my own who is *also* a dancin' man. That way, dancing would no longer be confined to official events. We could travel together and spontaneously "cut a rug" whenever the music moved us—in ballrooms and barrooms alike, in the streets, on the living room floor—anywhere. We'd practice to nail the fancier steps and he'd dip me dramatically at the perfect musical crescendoes, our bodies moving effortlessly in tandem like an amateur modern-day Fred-and-Ginger. The daydreaming came easily because it was *fun*. There was no doubt that my order had been taken by the Cosmic Waitress.

Somewhere along the line, though, I caught a nasty case of "what-is-itis." I started giving my attention to the idea that none of the dancing guys were "dating material," and that the men I *did* end up getting involved with were neither skilled at dancing nor very interested in learning. On the next deliberate Man-list I made, the criterion had shrunk to

118

merely "*open* to dancing," and even then I thought I was asking an awful lot in conjunction with the other items on the list. (Wrong! But we've already established that.)

Continuing my downhill slide into creation-by-oblivion, I further emphasized in my mind the division of "dancing guys" versus "datable guys" and naturally, was seeing more evidence of the divide as a result. Whenever I caught a live band at a small venue, some happy couple would inevitably take to the dance floor, smiling and sashaying about. I responded by turning on the self-pity channel and watching re-runs of "I'm all alone" and "I'll never find me a dancin' man," followed by an indignant "where's my stuff?" infomercial. I allowed the bitter taste of resentment to desecrate the inherent sweetness of the romantic scenes playing out before me.

Well, it took me a few years, but once I woke up from that victimhood slumber, I was able to change the channel. After that, when observing happy couples dancing together, I used the occasion to *fortify* my vision rather than blow it to bits. I imagined that I was the one being gleefully twirled about. Once I got started, the visualization gained momentum until the experience felt almost real.

I chatted with older couples who were in Love and had the sort of well-titrated dance chemistry I craved. As they talked lovingly about each other and their mutual passion for dancing, I imagined being them (or half of them), talking to a single gal. In other words, I conjured the feeling of being a supplier of inspiration, rather than the consumer I actually was at the moment. Let me tell you, that was a vibration makeover. Why? Giving just plum feels better than needing. To focus on what you have to give the world, rather than what you need to take from it, is to create an irrepressibly powerful magnetic field around you. Try it and you'll see what I mean.

Meanwhile, I took advantage of and relished whatever dance opportunities came my way. I even started proactively creating them. For example, at a gig that was normally poorly attended (and if anything, frequented by hippie noodle-dancers... *shudder*) I refused to go with pessimistic observations of the Past. Instead, I told myself that a swing dancer was going to show up. It worked. One time it was an 85-year-old man whose wife couldn't handle the faster moves, but hey, it was way better than no dancing. Besides, those older gentlemen are exceptionally skilled—they've had a few decades to practice.

Now that I'm with the Man of My Dreams, we're having fun dancing together. He came to me dance-ready, and although he needs further training, you won't find me complaining. (Hell, I could use a bit more training myself.) The joyful chemistry is there, just like I wanted.

It all works out in the end, but the quality of the journey is up to us. Why not make it your business to be happy, and to give freely of the Love you are seeking?

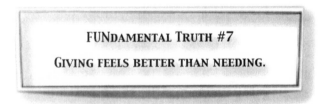

FUNDAMENTAL TRUTH #7

GIVING FEELS BETTER THAN NEEDING.

Potential inspiration is all around if you're open to it. The way we frame our experiences is everything. With dancing, I had two completely different emotional responses to nearly identical scenes. Which interpretation of reality produced greater happiness and expedited the MANifestation? The answer is obvious.

One day when I was walking around my cute little town, I spied a happy couple approaching on the sidewalk, holding hands and laughing. I smiled at them, and felt that giddy feeling of being in Love, knowing that I had my own Man waiting at home. What blew me away was that it was an exact carbon copy of an experience I'd had months *before* meeting Tony. When I was merely *pretending* to be hooked up while I walked, holding hands with my imaginary boyfriend, I generated a vibrational state *identical* to the physical reality that came later. The experience was striking —almost like déjà vu.

To the Universe, a well-done replica is as good as the real deal. Fake it as closely as you can, as often as you are able, and you will be pleasantly surprised with the results. The only caveat is that you want to stay motivated by the happiness and fun it provides for you in the Now, without being attached to any particular outcome in the Future. But that's actually much easier than it might sound since those good feelings are so addictive. And as you've probably gathered about my personal philosophy by now, *feeling good* is the Holy Grail.

In the Waiting Room

"Evil is boring. Cynicism is pointless. Fear is a bad habit. Despair is lazy. Hopelessness is self-indulgent. On the other hand: Joy is fascinating. Love is an act of heroic genius. Pleasure is our birthright. Chronic ecstasy is a learnable skill."
—*Rob Breszny*

Okay, so you're not *really* a lady-in-waiting, because you're busy living your life without regard to outcome and having a blast, correctamundo?

You've gotten clear about what you want. You may or may not be convinced that Mr. Right On is actually incarnate, but you know you're *worthy* of such a Man, if he does exist, and you're willing to play along with the idea that he does. You're spotting Resistance and Reactance and are actively changing your ways, developing new habits and forging new thought-pathways. You've done some belief inspection and releasing, and for the most part, you're feeling consistently happy. You're excited about meeting this Man of Your Dreams, but... *where the heck is he hiding?*

Your Man-dish definitely will be coming out of the Cosmic Kitchen (steaming hot!) but under no circumstances is it kosher for you to barge in there and micro-manage the chef. For the love of God, people, were you raised by wolves?! Learning to sit tight, amuse, soothe, and distract yourself while nibbling on crusts of bread is going to be your most valuable skill at this point.

Manifestations don't necessarily need to take *a lot* of time (unless, of course, we hold strong beliefs that they must). Mostly, the time required for materialization is the time it takes us to release enough Resistance to tip the scales of accumulated vibration. If you're doing all that you can to clean up your act but are still being kept waiting, then there's a good reason for it. It's all about *timing*, rather than time. Higher Mind is "waiting" for the perfect timing when all the cooperative components — people, situations, conditions, connections — are ideally aligned. Perhaps your Man recently got divorced and needs some alone-time to heal and polish himself up for you. Or he's about to move to your town from elsewhere. Or maybe there are some good reasons why you need to meet him at a specific event that hasn't taken place yet. These are the mysteries unknown and unknowable to the Physical Mind until after the fact.

All other factors aside, things rarely materialize *instantaneously* — at least not here in this time-space physical reality. (There are other realms of consciousness where thoughts immediately become "things," but that's another whole can of worms whose lid is better left on, methinks.) The built-in time lag — which some people claim has been getting progressively shorter for us — exists for our benefit, even though it can be frustrating at times. It gives us time to get our shit together in terms of our personal preferences and thought-emanations. And it's just another feature of the Earth game so, if at all possible, adopt a sporting attitude and drop the whiner routine.

When you get to the point where you enjoy complete and total faith in a forthcoming manifestation, then by all means, take Ernest Holmes' advice:

> *"Never let go of the mental image until it becomes manifested. Daily bring up the clear picture of what is wanted and impress it on the mind as an accomplished fact."*

In the meantime, and for the vast majority of us who are prone to meddling, it really is true that *letting go is the last step*. I'm sure you've heard it said many times that Love shows up after you've stopped looking. "Looking" too hard, in this sense, means attempting to force results by uninspired, calculated action—that is, Physical Mind-ing your way to the goods—or sadly, trying to alchemize brussels sprouts into chocolate cake again. That's the kind of feverish "looking" your need to cease and desist. A relaxed confident outlook is where it's at—staying open to inspired-action promptings from Higher Mind while holding positive *general* expectations.

It may be easier said and read than done firsthand, but take it from Yoda: *let go of control you must*. I also know how disheartened you may feel, hearing this part of the spiel, when you're nowhere near the vicinity of that requisite "letting go" mindset. It seems impossible in that moment, and any wise, well-intentioned counsel only flies in the face of your current experience. But remember, that's *all* it is: *current experience*. Everything in the Universe changes (except the Law of Attraction and the fact that you exist); therefore, your situation must change too.

It's going to happen in its own organic way—in its own divine timing. You can't forcibly fast-forward to the pivotal "letting go" moment in your story, as comically ironic as that would be. Doing the vibration clean-up work is the only fast track I know, because—and this is the sneaky part—it leads to you generating your bliss from within, rather than asking the "outside" world to give it to you. When you remain intrinsically happy most of the time, it's much easier to feel indifferent to specific outcomes. And when you're blissed out, you become a Love Magnet, pure and simple.

> ## MAN POINTER #5
>
> ### LETTING GO IS THE LAST STEP.

The Letting Go moment is the point where you *honestly* don't care anymore if, how, or when you meet the Man of Your Dreams. You're truly content in the Present moment, *needing* nothing additional or different in your reality. It's not that you stop *wanting* him—that would be lying to yourself. It's just that your *desire has been transformed and toned down from a burning need to a preference.* You no longer hold a stake in the outcome one way or another. You're reasonably happy, and you're sticking with the "this or something better" MANifesto while allowing Higher Mind to drive.

Even if you're feeling pessimistic at this juncture, there is still something you can do. The notion of letting go may be alien to you at the moment, but consider planting a seed in your mind that *it will happen* at some unknown point in the Future. In other words, entertain the idea that it *could* happen, despite the fact that you just can't see it from where you currently stand. Your ego-intellect may think this is pointless and overly simplistic, but trust me, it is not. There is far more power in subtlety and intention than there is in outward efforting. Besides, how many times have you experienced something in your life that you never imagined happening until it happened? There's your data, P-mind.

When you get to that "letting go" place, you will realize that the seed has germinated. You'll feel happy, but relatively neutral. Yes, you still have desires and preferences—you're alive and breathing, aren't you? It's just that you've removed *direness* from the equation, and that frees up a lot of energy that's convertible to pleasing manifestations. The funny thing is that, when they arrive, you're not quite as wowed as you once thought you'd be. I'm not saying you become jaded or anything, it's just that when your vibration has been consistently high for a while, the materialization of your desires seems more like a natural next step than a full-fledged jaw-dropping miracle. I suppose things just look different from various emotional altitudes.

My big Letting Go moment arrived about a month or so before I met Tony. I had been joyfully appreciating various Man-qualities in the world around me and applying all the other tricks in this book, and was humming along at a pleasantly even keel. But I still could not conceive of my "FrankenMan," so I figured that *maybe* I was going to live out the rest of my days as a single gal. I was fairly used to it, so it didn't strike me as a particularly awful sentence. I would simply continue having adventures, traveling and enjoying everyone and everything I encountered. Fine. But at times I also found myself thinking, *"hmmmm, I dunno, this shtick of mine is starting to get a little old."*

The crucial release came after those sorts of thoughts gathered steam, and I decided to have a little chat with my Higher Self. Well, alright, maybe it was closer to extortion. I contended that, even though I was committed to having fun here on Earth, I *do* get bored easily, and I always insist on having an out—say, at workshops or parties or whatever, if I decide it's not my thing. Since I know there is no such thing as *death*, the transition from physical to non-physical is the way we opt out of this Life phase and move on to the next. Basically, I issued an ultimatum, and I wasn't bluffing. It went something like this: "Look, if you've got some big plans for me that I'm unaware of, you had better send me a Man to co-create with, because if I decide I'm really over it, I will not hesitate to blow this popsicle stand."

It's not that I was plotting some sort of gruesome suicide, mind you. I'm way too squeamish and that would be paddling upstream, which is not at all my style. No, I just figured that when I'm done, I'll just *go*. Something will happen based on my free-will decision, the way many elderly people choose to exit in their sleep (it's just more socially acceptable when you're past a certain age).

You might find my outlook about Life and death to be odd, and that's fine, but the point is that *I genuinely let go*. Finally, the ball was fully in Higher Mind's court where it belongs. I decided, right then and there, that I would no longer engage in *wondering* whether or not my MANifestation might happen. In doing so, I released the final hold-out of Resistant thought, and the critical mass of positive thought-orders I'd been placing for many months quickly took effect. The floodgates were opened. Less than a month later, I met Tony. Voila.

There is no formula for letting go. You, too, will reach the point of release, by whatever means are necessary and relevant for *you*. It's a customized process that can't be controlled or predicted. So please, do yourself this favor: decide to *trust* that the timing and circumstances of your MANifestation will be perfect for you and for him, and allow the Universe—or challenge it, if that suits you better—to show you just how warranted your trust has been.

Practical Bliss

As you journey along, consider bringing Joseph Campbell as your travel buddy. Well, on second thought, just take his famous advice: *Follow Your Bliss*. Better still, forget about the *pursuit* of happiness—nab it already.

Many people, when they hear "follow your bliss," get immediately caught up in large sweeping thoughts about their lives, such as quitting a stable job to become an artist. This sort of overly broad thinking is bound to elicit a negative emotional backlash. That's because it is *unmanageable* from the Physical Mind perspective. P-mind wants to figure out all the interim steps to the big goal, but P-mind is not even *capable* of such an endeavor. P-mind only knows about the Past. Something brand new has no precedent, and therefore, no data. So the person gets scared and takes no action.

The secret to successful navigation of bliss is this (borrowed from a 1970s Steve Martin routine): *let's get small*. Think "next step on the footpath," not "next thousand miles on the superhighway." P-mind can take small steps, one foot after the other, but H-mind has the trail map and compass.

As physical beings, our best approach to overall bliss and materialization of our desires is to re-train ourselves in the Art of Following our Highest Micro-Excitement. We do this by choosing the more exciting action *in each moment*—no matter how small—given the options that are available to us in that moment. *Allow the macro-developments to unfold*. Manifestation is a magical daisy-chain of moments, strung exquisitely together by H-mind and her pals, for the satisfaction of all.

Let's say, for example, that it's your day off and you have a few things to accomplish. You say to yourself, "hmmm... which one of these things is more appealing to me at this moment—doing the laundry or going grocery shopping?" You decide that you're more inclined to do the laundry, even though you had *planned* to go to the store first. You don't need a reason—you simply honor that gut feeling, that impulsive voice that answers "laundry" when you inquire. So you override your previous arbitrary plan that was designed by Physical Mind, and you go ahead and start doing the laundry.

Then you experience a sudden impulse to turn on the radio, and in acting on that excitement, you discover there is a special program on the air. It's a band you love, performing live in the studio—what a treat! A little later, it *feels* like it's the right time to take care of the grocery shopping, so you head out to the store, where you just *happen* to run into a friend who tells you about a theatrical event that's right up your alley.

You decide to attend the play, but you aren't able to get to the box office for another week. You worry that it will be sold out for your preferred date—the date your Physical Mind selected as the best day, based on its calculation of a few different factors—or that you'll be stuck with a crappy seat. Nevertheless, you go to the theatre as soon as you are able, and you buy a ticket for the next available show, brushing aside P-mind's objections and concerns.

The night of the performance, you arrive at the theatre, and make your way to the section and row printed on your ticket. But there is some sort of mix-up because someone is occupying your seat. She's a bit pushy, this "theatre squatter," and does not want to relinquish the spot. Your blood starts to boil momentarily. What to do: kick her out, or just take a nearby open seat that was probably officially hers? You decide to let her stay put—because it's the path of least Resistance. You decide to let it go, sit down in the other row, and check out the program.

Five minutes later, a smiling man sits down next to you. He strikes up a conversation, and by the end of the night he's asking for your number. This charming fellow is later revealed to be the Man of Your Dreams. And all because you learned to follow your micro-excitement and chill the fuck out. Wow!

Yes, it *can* happen that smoothly. Things can happen like this all the time, if you simply *allow* for it. Your life can become a series of ecstatic synchronicities, much like that famous character in *The Celestine Prophecy*.

When you realize that everything is divinely orchestrated, you don't even get mad at the rascals anymore —like the ornery woman in the theatre—because you presume that they, like everyone and everything else in the Universe, are co-conspirators for your happiness. Just don't blame them if you don't like the results, because after all, they're just actors playing roles. *You*, my dear, are the script-writer of this play otherwise known as your life.

In addition to acting on your micro-excitement, it behooves you to *forgo* activities where your true excitement is absent. If you do something just because Physical Mind has determined it should lead to a particular outcome— such as meeting men—it's likely that you are generating Resistance by insisting that things must happen in a certain way and/or by becoming attached to outcome then getting upset when it doesn't happen that way. You're squeezing out possibilities better left to Higher Mind.

To borrow from some Ben & Jerry's bumper sticker philosophy, "If it's not fun, why do it?"

Do stuff you love whenever possible. That way it's easier to be happy, regardless of who does or doesn't show up.

Not to fuel any attachments to outcome here, but you probably noticed that I met my Man while I was doing one of my favorite things—woo-woo experiential learning. In the preceding fictional story, you were excited about the theatre, so that was a natural place for you and your Man to cross paths. My real-world friends Dave and Erika have a mutual love of nature, and that's what led each of them to join a group hike in the wilderness where they met and fell madly in love. Another happy couple I know, Julie and Steve, met in a dance class, having each heeded their personal excitement to learn tango.

Another pair of lovebirds I know met at a baseball game, when Cathy sold her extra ticket to John outside the stadium. He was instantly smitten but she was disinterested, and quickly walked away after completing the transaction. But his seat was adjacent to hers, and before the end of the game he succeeded in winning her over. Many years later, they're still together—married and making babies.

Our stories are as diverse as our personalities. No matter what the particulars of yours turn out to be, if you make a point of following that trail of popcorn laid out for you by Higher Mind, crunching one mouthful of bliss at a time, you most definitely *will* have a fun Love Story to tell. And a major chapter is going to be about aligning with self-love.

Get into some juicy moment-to-moment living. And for the love of god, stop meddling! You don't want to get so close to your MANifestation only to have him slip away, with the Universe mumbling, Scooby Do villain style, "I would've gotten away with it, if it weren't for those meddling kids..."

Kidding! Don't worry. Be happy, dammit.

Miscellaneous Tools and Tips
for MANifesting and general vibrational bliss

1. Go, go, Gadget.

Set your phone or computer or other gadget to remind you throughout the day to check in with your thoughts and feelings. It's too easy to slip back into auto-pilot mode. There are several apps out there to assist you in staying on track, so if you're a gadget-gal, why not make use of them?

2. Good ol' Swear Jar.

Years ago, I lived in a big house with several housemates, and we'd often spontaneously enact some sort of fun creative project. One of these was the Swear Jar—not for ordinary curse words though, because where's the fun in that? No, this jar had a custom menu of terms and how much each utterance would cost you. "Pregnant" had a high price tag, as did "Kenny Loggins" but "can't" brought in the most cash for our party fund. If you live or work with others who might play along, this is a light-hearted way to retrain yourself to stop saying negative unhelpful things.

3. Ask, don't tell.

Get in the habit of asking questions, rather than making statements, because it leaves room for answers to come. For example, when I say "where is my camera?" or "how can I find my camera?" then I'll locate it much sooner than if I proclaim "I can't find my camera." We're unconditionally supported by the Universe, so if I state that I can't find it, the response is "okay, you can't find your camera. Your wish is my command." So in that spirit, stating "I am finding my camera... ", though not a question, is a helpful variation.

It's more about attitude and vibration than words. The difference is fairly evident: in asking, the mood is more curious, inquisitive, open to possibilities, and skewed toward positive expectation. When making definitive statements, the vibration is usually more dense, closed, inflexible, and often sprinkled with annoyance or other negative Reactance. It is our Resistance to "what-is" that holds us there.

4. Be solution-oriented.

I know that sounds like one of those rah-rah (or blah-blah-blah) motivational platitudes, but it's actually very simple and practical. Any problem and its solutions are on completely different wavelengths. So when you're consumed by the problem, you are *of* the problem vibration, so you simply do not have access to solutions. That is, you cannot *perceive* a solution, and the situation looks pretty impossible to resolve. That's not the whole truth, but it *seems* that way as long as you're locked into the problem vibe.

Here's what you can do: simply *think* the word "solution." Just entertain the idea of it—roll the word around for a minute. Ask, "what is the solution here?" rather than using your precious energy to report on the status of "what-is" by stating "this isn't working" or "this sucks." Thinking about the *mere idea of a solution* is a foot in the door, and that's all you need at first. Then, when curiosity usurps fear, marked changes occur.

5. Go-to gimmick.

You might find it helpful to have some vibration-changing trick at the ready—a purposeful action to take when you notice an old negative pattern creeping in. It could be something specific and physical, like drinking water or rolling your eyes upward (which sounds dumb but the motion has been linked to alpha wave brain activity). Or shifting to your "happy place" with go-to subjects or photographs—kittens, puppies, babies, whatever works for you. Maybe it's remembering that triumphant day back in fourth grade when you won the spelling bee. Don't worry about it being stupid or corny—no one else needs to know.

I often employ song snippets (or, I suppose Higher Mind plants them in my mind's ear). For instance, "it won't mean a thing in a 100 years..." or "gotta lighten up right now" (Blues Traveler, and the Beastie Boys, respectively). The Jeffersons' theme song ("movin' on up...") has shown up as a benevolent earworm at times. Hey, look, I'm not proud. Anything that amounts to a vibrational foot-in-the-door is going to help you switch tracks and rewire those neural brain networks for positivity.

6. Deep in the heart of Woo-Woo

If you're inclined to meditate and experiment with energy and color, here's an interesting exercise I picked up somewhere along the way. Imagine your heart center consumed in a violet flame, and connect it to your Man's heart as you watch the flame grow. Notice what happens... things could get *very* interesting.

A simpler take on this is to get relaxed, then imagine your Man in some energetic sense (the idea of him is enough), and simply say "I Love You." On some level, he's going to feel your telempathic message and feel all warm and fuzzy inside, so you might want to note the date and time for comparing notes with him later on.

7. Feng Shui and other Permission Slips.

I dig the Feng Shui. Playing with colors, shapes and symbols while re-decorating the house is my idea of a good time. You betcha, I fancied up the Love Corners in my place, put tables on both sides of the bed, made space in the closet for him (well, nature *does* abhor a vacuum) and everything else I read about that sounded like a good idea.

The *real power* lies within our consciousness, of course. We can attribute power to "outside" objects, rituals, or other people, but it's just a permission slip to feel good and therefore allow manifestations to materialize. The same goes for collages or vision boards. We do the "work" with our minds, and the art is there to inspire and re-mind us. Now, that's not to say there's anything *wrong* with permission slips. Hell no, they're great! We all use them.

I like using astrological analysis to understand a lot of things, including interpersonal dynamics, but I've also used it as a permission slip to believe that certain relationships were more doable than they actually were. I was looking at a narrow, distorted subset of the data because I chose to delude myself at the time. The tool is objective, but it's how we wield it that matters most.

Anyway, my point is that any tool can work for or against your best interests. So, by all means, make use of anything that assists you in feeling more confident, happy and powerful, but be sure to also give yourself *permission* to abandon those things, if and when the time comes.

8. AffirmMantras

I have to put in another plug for old-school affirmations because it's such good stuff. If you brushed off the suggestion last time, you might want to actually do it now. Record yourself saying positive things and listen to it two or three times a day. You will notice some changes almost immediately. Of course, the conscious mind balks at the statements initially, because they don't *feel* true. Well, of course they don't! You're planting a new seed here and mustering a new vibration. Are you going to allow yourself to be shut down *that easily* by the ego-intellect? A seed doesn't usually quantum-jump into a full-grown tree bearing fruit. You might want to to give it a minute.

You may also want to use affirmations like mantras to counteract negative thoughts directly after they occur.

9. Test Drive the Law of Attraction

Actually, you've been working with the Law of Attraction your entire life, as have all of us. But in this hazy atmosphere of intellectual doubt, a gal can stand a little reinforcing. Since no one can "prove" to you that the Law of Attraction is in effect, proving it to yourself is crucial. For this reason, I keep an LOA jar of scribbled manifestation stories. "Open in case of doubt," it says. It could be a notebook just the same, but you get the idea.

Probably you can recall examples from your Past, but you might also want to start some new deliberate manifesting projects—"small" things that have no emotional charge associated with them. Some people play the "Manifestation of the Day" game with friends, texting each other the chosen target, and then the results. Practice targets are usually simple and iconic: zebras, feathers, gold stars, blue fish, etc. Use your imagination. Enlist co-conspirators if possible—it's more fun and exciting that way. Whatever you pick, the key to working with intention is "set it and forget it." Keep yourself busy and don't obsess over it. It will show up in your experience in delightful ways that exceed statistical odds and bolster your faith in LOA.

10. Tell me a story...

One of my favorite things to do is ask happy couples how they met. I do it because I'm in love with Love and with people and their stories, but it has some other specific benefits that might interest you. First, it reminds you of the great diversity in which the Universe thrives, appeasing the Physical Mind by providing a tiny sampling of possibilities for uniting a righteous loving pair of humans. Second, it tends to bring out a spark in *them* as they recount happy, humorous memories together. And lastly, it's highly entertaining for all when you ask each partner separately and get two very different perceptions of the same events.

It's a simple pastime that costs nothing and engenders an abundance of good feelings. Oftentimes, we get immersed in our own Drama and forget to connect with others, so this is one way to extract your head from your rear-end, if that's where it's been hiding.

11. Put your mind on a diet.

Give the 7-Day Mental Diet a whirl. I believe the idea was originated by Emmet Fox about a century ago, and it's brilliantly simple: for an entire week, do not entertain negative thoughts of any kind. We're talking fear, anger, criticism, doubt, worry, resentment, etc. That leaves you with things like love, appreciation, amusement, acceptance, curiosity, positive anticipation and allowing.

The concept of "entertaining" is key. Yes, of course, negative thoughts are going to show up; there's no denying that, even for the cleanest, leanest mind on the Planet. But like an unwelcome solicitor at the front door, you don't want to invite them in and serve them tea and cookies. As soon as you recognize a not-so-helpful thought-form, you set it free.

In its purest design, the diet has a zero tolerance policy.

Talk about a challenging Olympic sport! If you succeed—and I say success is defined by the individual—or even if you don't, you're going to gain something valuable from the experience. Besides, it requires no special training, no money, no cooperation from others—nothing other than your resolve and intention. So what have you got to lose, besides emotional baggage?

12. This here crazy web.

No, not the Interweb—the *other* crazy web. The part where we're all interconnected. Just as there are cooperative components to realizing *your* desires—such as the nameless woman at the salon who mentions a book that rocks your world... or the tree that falls on your car, sending you to the body shop where you meet the Man of Your Dreams—*you, too, are a cooperative component for others.* We don't always consciously know the roles we play, but whenever I get an inside peek at the co-creative process, it just tickles me.

One day I was working steadily for hours on my computer when I felt a sudden urge to go check the mail. It was a little bit of a walk to the mailbox and a storm was brewing outside, but I honored the impulse anyway. Well, the mailbox was empty, but as I turned back, a man approached, calling out to me. He had come to visit my neighbor, but since he was visually impaired and now utterly lost in our illogically laid-out complex, he had just about given up. He seemed greatly relieved as I escorted him to his destination. These sorts of experiences fortify our understanding of and reverence for the mechanics of this amazing Universe. Be on the lookout for them!

Recommending Reading

Since every waiting room has reading materials, here are some of my favorites for you to thumb through:

If the Buddha Dated by **Charlotte Kasl** is a potent little purse-sized collection of practical wisdom. *If the Buddha Married* is also quite good.

Mama Gena's School of Womanly Arts: Using the Power of Pleasure to Have Your Way with the World, by **Regena Thomashauer**, takes a look at handling the gender divide in a light-hearted, playful, and very smart way.

The Four Man Plan by **Cindy Lu** is not only hilarious and clever, but it can actually help call off the dogs of female obsession by dispersing your dating energy—all this while spurring you on to greater self-love. Such a bargain.

Marianne Williamson's classic, *A Return to Love*, is an inspiring, no-nonsense interpretation of *A Course in Miracles*. *A Woman's Worth* is a more sober pick—thought-provoking and potentially healing—and a good one for exploring a longer view of women's empowerment.

Your Heart's Desire by **Sonia Choquette** is a great straightforward manifesting manual. Sweetly inspiring.

Shakti Gawain's *Creative Visualization* has been an old friend for decades. Pocket-sized, tried and true.

When it comes to mastering your emotional terrain, *Ask and It Is Given* by **Esther and Jerry Hicks** is chock full of practical ways to pull your vibrations (gently) up by their proverbial bootstraps.

If you happen to be a complete LOA newbie, check out **Michael Losier**'s simplified take on things, aptly named *The Law of Attraction*. Back to basics.

If you're keenly interested in energetic self-healing, then *Chakras For Beginners: A Guide to Balancing Your Chakra Energies* by **David Pond** and *Your Aura & Your Chakras: The Owner's Manual* by **Karla McLaren** are excellent. Interestingly, Ms. McLaren has since forsaken her woo-woo phase, but that doesn't negate the usefulness of her seminal work for the rest of us.

For boundless comedy and tough-love truth about discerning shit from shinola, be sure to check out *He's Just Not That Into You* by **Greg Behrendt** and **Liz Tuccillo**. Hysterical, but possibly hard-hitting—you've been warned.

If you aren't particularly freaked out by the idea of a thunderous-voiced extra-terrestrial from the Future channeled through a bald dude wearing a Hawaiian shirt, do investigate the brilliant physics and personal empowerment teachings of **Bashar** and **Darryl Anka**.

Lastly, though it's not a book, **Sean Hayes**' original music is highly plug-worthy. The guy is seriously talented. Check him out at: www.SeanHayesMusic.com.

Abiding thanks to all my teachers, both overt and inadvertent.

FROM HOOKING UP

to shacking up

"Joy is what happens when we allow ourselves to recognize how good things are. Joy is not necessarily what happens when things unfold according to our own plans."
—Marianne Williamson

❤

In a modern adaptation of fairytale legend,

Tony rode up in a white Chevy van, having driven intransigently westward for days toward the sunset and me. The man had made up his mind, and there was no obstacle even mildly capable of thwarting him now. He called regularly from the road, crazy with purpose and fueled by a potent mix of testosterone, nicotine, adrenaline and coffee.

He was headed my way, that was for certain, but for how long and exactly how it was all going to work, I had no idea. But then, I wasn't feeling much of a need to ask questions. All I knew was that my relationship back-order had finally been filled, and I was about to take delivery of the goods.

Two solid months of long distance courtship had brought us closer together than he'd ever been with a girl. Yeah, that's right, I said "girl." He's old school like that, and uses that word to describe anyone of the female persuasion, whether she's six or sixty. It's amusing to notice that what deeply offended me twenty years ago I now find exceptionally cute and endearing.

It was Friday evening when he arrived on my doorstep. I have to admit, it felt a little odd. When he kissed me, he was once again a stranger, and I recoiled ever so slightly. Our lengthy conversations had bonded us psychologically, but I guess I needed to rekindle that lovin' feeling in the flesh. Maybe it's a chick thing, or just my own peculiar brand of Venus-in-Pisces fickleness. Whatever it was, it didn't last very long. My ambivalence was no match for his exuberance.

That first night together was sweet, but anticlimactic. Our self-induced hype and imaginings of reunion sex had built up pressure; we ended up drinking too much and falling asleep.

As the weekend progressed, things improved rapidly. I had stocked up on various decadent treats, so we had everything we needed: food, music, candles and each other. Plus there were lovely environs for taking a walk—if and when we were to venture outside. What else mattered? It was one of those magical dates that lasts an entire weekend —the kind that immerses you in an altered reality bubble built for two. That is, until Monday comes. But in our case, Monday was of no consequence, because neither of us had anything particularly pressing to attend to.

Mondays came and Mondays went, and there we were, living together—blissfully, for the most part. Sane people usually date each other for a while before cohabitating, but I suppose sanity is better left for the sane. A friend of mine half-jokingly suggested that I write a book called "How to Move In With Your Boyfriend for Dummies." I thought about it for a minute but decided I was better qualified to write one titled, "How *Not to* Move In With Your Boyfriend: Don't be a Dumb-Ass."

After a few weeks, "blissful for the most part" living became "often blissful... and occasionally agitated" living. Yes, my buttons were getting pushed. And it's no wonder, considering I'd been living alone for many years. But that's the celebrated utility of an intimate relationship—it impels you to take out the trash, and face the truth about yourself. The efficiency can be mind-blowing.

Though our woo-woo world-views coincide beautifully, Tony and I were the classic Odd Couple in a domestic sense. Pack-a-day smokin', Walmart-shopping, classic rock listening T-rex meets eco-hippie, classic jazz aficionada, DIY, pseudo-foodie girl. He had never heard of such things as quinoa or yurts, didn't know a beet from a rutabaga, and had to be verily schooled in the basics of household trash recycling. I'd once set a "zero garbage" goal for myself and came pretty close to achieving it, and here I was with a man who goes through more paper towels in a week than I'd used in an entire decade. I, on the other hand, produced blank stares when he'd rattle off Hollywood movies and actors' names. I made no attempt to conceal my scorn for his "inferior" consumerist choices.

Our culture clash had another element: divergent upbringings. Though we both hail from somewhat dysfunctional families (and who doesn't, really?), I come from a long line of uptight, northern European, sober Protestant types while he's working with a decidedly Mediterranean palette of expression. He's loud; I get concerned about annoying the neighbors. I get myself wound up too tightly if it seems we're running late; he assumes everything will work out fine (it does). He does everything on a grand scale with total abandon—like using every dish and utensil in the kitchen. I tend to conserve and ration, plan and plot... and tense up.

All this tough love from the Universe, just when I thought I had nothing left in common with my bio-family.

Speaking of child-rearing, I like to joke that I was raised by Virgos. It's kind of like being raised by wolves, only neater and more anal-retentive. As it turns out, Virgosity comes in many flavors. My friend Lucy used to say that "some people are Neatniks and some are Cleanniks." I suppose I'm a little of both, despite the fact that I haven't got much Virgo in my natal astrology chart to call my own. Call me a poser, but I just like things the way I like them. Sure, sometimes I let things get messy, but since it's *my* mess, I'm usually okay with it for a while. Other people's messes in my space are somehow far less tolerable.

Enter Virgo Man. The good news is that he compulsively makes the bed every day—even twice a day if I mess it up with a midday nap—and he can't stand the sight of dirty dishes hanging around. But his fastidiousness started driving me up the wall because no sooner would I set down a water glass than it got spirited away to the sink. And it didn't seem to matter to him if things actually got very clean —as long as they *looked* a certain way. *Ahh, I see I've got a Neatnik on my hands.*

Then there was the usual gender-divide household comedy, like him leaving the toilet seat up and me nagging him not to. (Hint: nagging is not actually helpful.) Or my perturbation at his man-vision that only penetrates an inch or two of the refrigerator.

I obviously had to make some adjustments. I won't say sacrifices, because it's helped me become more of my true self. Believe it or not, I don't actually prefer being judgmental, persnickety, or anything else that interferes with Romance.

My annoyance actually led to some potent realizations. I needed to confront my superfluous concern for other people's opinions, for one thing. And my vestigial beliefs in scarcity—that was a big nugget of un-inspected belief system territory. I'd inherited the conservative ways of my kin, but never actually stopped to ponder whether those beliefs belonged to me or not. I was a "belief thief," as Bashar says playfully. My beloved great-grandmother's motto was: "Use it up, wear it out, make it do or do without." Not exactly an affirmation of prosperity and abundance, eh?

I had to hone my conflict resolution skills, big time. Initially, when my buttons were pushed, I found myself sucked in to The Drama. My ego was insisting that I must have my way, and my Physical Mind was predicting a Future of unhappiness based on the current data. That kind of tag team effort packs a wallop. But I snapped out of it, thank goodness—and realized it was all very purposeful.

It sure didn't hurt that this sweet, beautiful man cooked for me every day and loved me unconditionally, despite my occasional temper tantrums. And when he unpacked his books—his most prized possessions—revealing titles like *How to Stay in Love* and *The One Hour Orgasm*, along with an impressive assortment of woo-woo reading, I got a needed nudge. *Oh…right! He's the Man of My Dreams. I can stop playing SuperBitch now.*

I just had some "stuff" to work through. Most of us do. There's a solution for every conflict. It's just that, while I was in an emotional funk, I only had access to the problems. Naturally, the more I focused on annoyances, the more I saw of them. And the more I reacted to them, the farther I was from the vibration of the solutions. I can honestly say that falling off the positivity wagon like that was, ironically, a very positive thing for me because once I emerged from my stupor I understood the Law of Attraction and the emotional guidance system more solidly than ever before.

I think the big breakthrough came when Tony and I decided to do the 7-Day Mental Diet together. I committed to casting off all negative thoughts. The next time I went in the bathroom and found the toilet seat up, rather than griping and wondering if the man would ever become fully potty-trained, I deliberately shifted to Appreciation. *"Oh, there's a sign that Tony's been here,"* I thought. *"I love that guy."* It may sound petty, but it was huge. With that, I began a new emotional trajectory. And he rarely left the seat up again, because I no longer had Reactance and Resistance to it. See? This stuff works.

And so it goes. What doesn't kill your love affair only makes it stronger. The truth is, Tony and I are superb complements: our differences are really assets. That was easy to see after I took out the head-trash. (Hmmm, now there's a great idea—setting a zero "mind-garbage" goal!) It just goes to show how our emotional state of mind filters perception. Focusing on the good stuff actually *does* cause the unsavory parts to fade into the background, but when I was drunk on the Drama, like most drunks, I was incapable of doing a good job. Thankfully, those dramatic passages became shorter and less frequent, and now I can spot them coming miles away—and abate the damage.

The communication and compassion I've cultivated with Tony will carry us through any hiccups that arise, because I can be real in his presence. In fact, I *need* to be real in his presence, and that is what makes him the Man of My Dreams, above all.

Everything changes and gets better, especially since I stopped insisting that it wouldn't or couldn't. We've returned to the caliber of fun we had during that magical first week at the Monroe Institute. He constantly cracks me up and never ceases to impress me with his loving, thoughtful, creative ways. We're happily, goofily envisioning, co-creating, and converting our dreams to waking reality. The man eventually started eating vegetables and even quit smoking. And as for me, well I'm learning to chill out—to accept, love and trust even more... and also to *receive* more readily. How does it get any better than that?

So, maybe shacking up is part of *your* personal vision, and maybe it isn't. It pays to be clear and honest with yourself about what you really want, and why you want it.

Once upon a time, I used to admire couples who lived apart, thinking they were very smart to retain their individuality that way. But I've come to realize that more togetherness is what I actually prefer, and Higher Mind has connected me to the right Man who makes it all work. We're close *and* we have our individual freedom. And why shouldn't we? That was just a limiting thought from a Physical Mind saying it had to be one *or* the other, not both.

Both is what you want. And both is what you will get if you don't cling to those confining "either/or" belief systems. Having your cake and eating it too is how Life was meant to be. Everything is possible. And the things we want the most are not only possible, they're highly *probable*.

Every experience is an opportunity to sharpen our comprehension of Universal Law, and make use of our personal toolkits to practice greater *allowing*. Falling off the wagon is hardly grounds for self-reproach; it's a necessary part of the Earth School curriculum, and it easily becomes fodder for joyful expansion if you allow it to be.

In wrapping up this little Love Story, I send some extra love out to you along with this postulate: each moment is a new manifestation, and so we strive to become increasingly conscious in the molding of our thought-creations. But equally important is that we remain forever gentle with ourselves.

FAQ
Frequently Acquired Quandaries

Q. What if the Man of My Dreams is married?

A. Is "married" on your Man-list? I didn't think so. Is he *really* the Man of Your Dreams, or are you trying to talk yourself into it? Do you realize you can conjure another Man with all of his desirable qualities and without the vexing one that requires you to compromise yourself in unwanted ways? Even if you believe in karmic bonding, you can now choose to believe that you have the power to terminate contracts that no longer serve you. Inspecting and releasing your beliefs that cause you to define pain as pleasure, contrary to your conscious logical understanding, is likely to catalyze some desirable changes. Well, whatever you do, please don't beat yourself up. After all, it's just another experience to have while playing the Earth game.

Q. I read your woo-woo book and nothing's happening—I think you're full of shit.

A. Awesome! Gotta love diversity. Why some people dive into this self-empowerment stuff while others sit on the sidelines is a mystery, probably known only to the Higher Mind that holds the road map. For those who *do* apply the information and get results, reading is "necessary but not sufficient," as they say in Logic jargon. If you genuinely want your situation to change, you must actively change yourself by altering your thoughts and beliefs. I suspect you're giving up too easily. And the assertion that "nothing's happening" is evidence of that all-too-common form of Resistance known as "weh! where's my stuff?!" Other people and books can help you to re-mind yourself, but ultimately you have to dive in and do the personal work. There is no magic pill or silver bullet. You can use me as an excuse for holding tight to your Resistance if you like, but that doesn't really further your cause, right? When you're able to wrestle the ego-intellect to the ground, that's when some real change is possible.

Q. **Self-deprecating humor is an integral part of my personality. I'm afraid if I stop doing that, I'll become some watered-down, hearts-and-smileys goody-two-shoes New Ager. I just can't risk that.**

A. Refusing to take the reins of your own reality experience because other people who do it (or at least talk about it) are annoying amounts to what is known as "cutting off the nose to spite the face." Here's an idea: why not give yourself more credit? Things don't need to be so black-and-white. There are infinite possibilities. So anyway, *are* self-deprecatory jokes really injurious to your Man-plan? Maybe? Probably. The thing is, words can deceive, and as their purveyor, only *you* know what's underneath them. I'm going to go out on a limb here and suggest that there is genuine feeling behind your jokes though, because as they say, there's always a certain percentage of truth in comedy (and that's what makes it funny). I suppose it all comes down to this: what's more important —upholding your old self-image, or mama gettin' some? The best answer is *both*. With a little creative tweaking, you really *can* have it all. And if you *do* decide to quit the self-sabotaging circuit, it sounds like you'll have plenty of new comedic fodder because you can make fun of yourself for becoming a sell-out. And let's face it, finding humor in New Agey stuff is like shooting fish in a barrel.

Q. I had the Man of My Dreams already, but he's gone... and there will never be another.

A. Well, okay, if you insist. We all have our stories that we benefit from retelling. But maybe you actually *do* want another round at the Man-table? If it's just a matter of semantics, call him something else, I dunno, like your new Man-friend or something. That way he won't be taking anything away from the memories and the story you cherish. It's all about your beliefs and definitions, and you're the boss. You can tell a new story or modify your story any time, and you can create another relationship of whatever variety you like. You just need to come clean with yourself and your true desires.

Q. The Man of My Dreams is someone famous... but I doubt I'll ever actually meet him.

A. Okay, so first of all, this celebrity is unlikely to be the Man of Your Dreams because you don't really know him —you're just projecting stuff onto him. Not impossible, because nothing is, but nonetheless *unlikely*. The good news is that you can harness your powerful imagination to work *for* you. Focus on the qualities you believe this Man has, while allowing Higher Mind to decide on the particular *form* through which it delivers those *essences* or aspects of your MANifestation. You can still use his qualities to visualize, but just reinforce the idea that "this or something better" is coming to you now. And please decide to stop saying or thinking "I doubt I'll ever meet him" because that Resistance doesn't serve you. When you stop insisting on the exact *form* that your MANifestation must take (as a particular person), then the doubting subsides naturally. Also, look for beliefs that keep you unavailable to be in an actual relationship.

Q. I've been trying really hard, but I'm still just seeing the same old stuff—guys who are broke, unattractive, etc.

A. That old adage, "a watched pot never boils" comes to mind. Likely, you are quick to notice that you're still at Point A while anxious to be at Point B. Thoughts like "nothing's changing... guys are broke" are Resistant. These things take persistence—particularly when you're dealing with belief systems around money and self-esteem. You can view this "waiting period" as an opportunity to investigate your beliefs while detaching from the MANifestation outcome. The world is a giant mirror, so low-cash-flow dudes show you valuable information about *your own* attitudes toward money. Sorry if the project's turning out to be more elaborate than anticipated, but I assure you, the investment in yourself is well worth the effort, both for you and for the Man of Your Dreams who is en route.

Q. I'm feeling twitterpated about this Man of My Dreams thing, but also scared that so many months after we hook up, he'll die... or that I'll want to kill him.

A. Great news! You've identified your fears. Now you know what sort of Resistance is ready to be released. Aren't you the efficient one?! Well, if you *know* that you create your own reality, it doesn't make much sense to fear that something unwanted will occur, right? The only way it can occur is if you keep focusing energy on it with repetitive thoughts and emotion. Now that you've identified a theme, you can choose to change. It's all up to you. And with that kind of awareness, you're well on your way to having things go your way. Bravo! Enjoy the twitterpation.

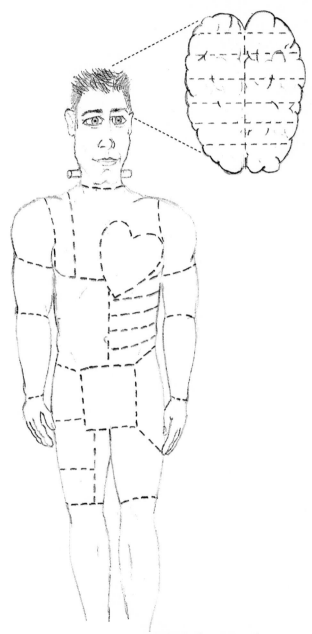

Active Appreciating

Today, I will notice and appreciate pleasing qualities in the world around me, especially in any men I encounter, see, hear, or hear about. I will do my noticing in an organic fashion without scheming, plotting, or fretting. I just intend... and see what happens. This is fun!

Man-list Item 1: _____

Scenario 1: _____

_____

Scenario 2: _____

_____

Scenario 3: _____

_____

Man-list Item 1: _____

Scenario 1: _____

_____

Scenario 2: _____

_____

Scenario 3: _____

_____

Man-list Item 1: _____

Scenario 1: _____

_____

Scenario 2: _____

_____

Scenario 3: _____

_____

© 2015 Debbianne DeRose

If all else fails, head down to the local hardware store
and get yourself a studfinder.

Please share *your* juicy MANifestation stories at
www.debbianne.com

Debbianne DeRose was formally trained in the Conservative Arts of engineering and economics and enjoyed stints as enginerd, database geek, non-profiteer, college instructor, bricolage artist and inadvertent house flipper before diving headlong into the world of woo-woo wordsmithery. She resides in the San Francisco Bay Area with the Man of Her Dreams, where she can swim regularly in the seas of Woo, buoyed always by her Jersey girl sensibilities and sense of humor. After all, there's nothing *serious* going on here.

Please visit **Debbianne.com** for thought-provoking, giggle-inducing angles on this Universe thingy we're living in.

Praise for
What I Did On My Midlife Crisis Vacation
by Debbianne DeRose

"I must say that this is the funniest book ever! It's the book that you and your friends will be passing around and talking about all year long!" — Rita Reviews

"Vibrant, alive and real, written by someone who has experienced life in the new. A must read for spiritual like minded people." — LL Book Review

"Plenty of humor and plenty to ponder... a strong pick." — Midwest Book Review

"Debbianne has hit a spiritual nerve here...which seems also to connect to the funny bone. She sifts through many paradigms to clarify her own truth about the nature of our reality and she wears the hats of neophyte, old soul, skeptic, and choir member with equal ease. She is a New Age traveler channeling Erma Bombeck." — Bruce Barth

"DeRose gives voice to many of the same concerns other midlifers may be too afraid to admit... and quickly diffuses any fear with her wacky humor." — Reader Views

"I'm still thinking about the issues in this book, and this is definitely one I will be reading again. I learned a lot about myself..." — Melissa's Midnight Musings

"I will never feel alone again in my wanting a connection to the divine. Debbianne's down-to-earth, humorous insights released the spiritual tension often felt by those who go in search of the meaning of life." — Jenni Joy, Step Lightly blog

"I enjoyed the way she sets about telling her story like a friend updates you after an extended break, with commonsense and humour—bucket loads of it. Debbianne's quest to become a clairvoyant, to experience life-changing moments of spirituality, was fascinating to read." — Read Reviewed

"She has exactly the right balance of skepticism and open-mindedness to make the writing have universal appeal, however much the reader personally believes in all that woo." — Madhouse Reviews

The Man of YOUR Dreams awaits...

enjoy the journey.

CPSIA information can be obtained at www.ICGtesting.com
Printed in the USA
LVOW130110170113

315631LV00001BA/2/P

9 780985 410131